33 WAYS NOT TO SCREW UP TEACHING ADULTS TO READ

JOANNE TELSER-FRÈRE

ISBN: 978-1-955750-91-2 - eBook

ISBN: 978-1-955750-92-9 - Print

Contents

Introduction

I fell into teaching in the 1970s. It was pure chance that led me there. I had no professional education or experience in the field, but I had a Bachelor's degree from the University of Illinois' College of Arts and Sciences. I was living in France and was hired to teach English to adults. Although I lacked teacher training and had doubts, it was a blessing in disguise. I found that not knowing the "rules" of teaching was actually beneficial. Through experimentation and various training courses, I taught myself how to teach and quickly discovered that my methods were effective.

Over the years, I became a specialist in adult education and taught worldwide, including Pakistan, Egypt, Qatar, France, and the United States. Although I primarily taught English as a second language (ESL), I also trained language teachers, taught brain training to seniors, citizenship to immigrants, and reading English to American adults with low literacy levels.

In addition to my teaching career, I also succeeded in Doha, Qatar, where I produced TV programs for both the English and French radio stations. Additionally, I wrote for the press. To round out my communication skills, I completed the Toastmasters Speaking and Leadership program twice, once in French and once in English.

Eventually, I found my way to Literacy Chicago in 2016, where I serve as Director of Program Development and Volunteer Management. Literacy Chicago is the oldest literacy organization in Chicago, founded in 1968. Only 15 organizations listed with the Secretary of State of Illinois do this type of work within the state. There are many more that work with children. Literacy Chicago's mission is to empower adults through education, a mission with which I am completely aligned. I have finally found my calling, and I hope this book will encourage others to recognize the importance of ensuring that every adult can read. My mission in writing this book is to suggest methods and tools to make this goal a reality.

33 Ways Not to Screw Up Teaching Adults to Read is not a list of things NOT to do as the title may suggest. It is tips, tricks, and thought-provoking ideas meant to help you be a successful and engaging teacher.

I hope you enjoy it!
Joanne Telser-Frère

Foreword

It is with great pleasure that I reflect on my friendship with Joanne Telser-Frère, a remarkable individual whom I have had the privilege of knowing since 2016. Initially, our relationship began within the professional realm when I engaged Joanne as an instructor for Literacy Chicago's citizenship program. However, over the years, our connection has blossomed into a cherished friendship.

In Joanne, I've witnessed an unwavering passion for teaching, especially within Chicago's adult education community. Her commitment and dedication to empowering individuals through education is truly inspiring.

Now, let's talk about "33 Ways Not to Screw Up Teaching Adults to Read." This guide isn't just another resource; it's a beacon of encouragement, inspiration, and insight for educators diving into the noble journey of teaching adults.

In the world of adult education, understanding the nuances, unique characteristics, and challenges of adult learners is key. This guide dives deep into their psyche, exploring behaviors, barriers, and everything in between. Through engaging exercises and observations, educators will gain valuable insights into their students' diverse experiences and needs.

As you flip through these pages, you'll explore practical literacy theories and their real-world applications in adult education. From making lessons relevant to adapting teaching methods, this guide serves as your roadmap for effective instruction.

I invite educators to dive in with an open mind and a hunger for knowledge. May this guide be your compass, guiding you through the intricate landscape of adult education and empowering you to make a meaningful impact in your students' lives.

Joanne's wealth of experience spans decades and extends across various corners of the globe, making her contributions to adult education invaluable. At Literacy Chicago, we're lucky to have her on our team. Her innovative programs and genuine support for our students leave a lasting mark.

Reflecting on Joanne's journey fills me with admiration and gratitude for her tireless work in advancing adult education in our community. Let this guide spark a passion for learning in you, fostering a culture of understanding and paving the way for lifelong education.

Richard Dominguez | Executive Director, Literacy Chicago

1

Words Around Us

UNDERSTAND WHAT ADULTS WITH LOW LITERACY LEVELS DON'T SEE

If you are reading these words, you are literate. Most likely, when you walk down the street, you notice all kinds of words without realizing it. Just think about it for a moment. There are street signs and signs on shops, banks, and hospitals. There are road signs, parking rules, and "Sidewalk Closed" signs. Restaurants advertise their menus, grocery stores tout their sales, and fast-food places post drive-through menus. There are bus signs, train signs, and even graffiti.

For those of us who are literate, it is hard to imagine life without being able to read and comprehend the written word without giving it a second thought. However, according to data published by the US Department of Education, for 43 million adults with low literacy levels, that is more or less their reality.[1] Although more than half of these 43 million can successfully determine the meaning of sentences, read relatively short texts to locate a single piece of information, or complete simple forms, it is a constant struggle.

People who don't read well often don't pay attention to all the words around them. Some words will jump out, the ones they know. They might see "Stop," "Sale," or "Parking"- and then again, they might not. There could be some recognizable trademark words. Just google "Coke logos around the world" and see how many you can easily identify.

Imagine walking down a street in a country where the alphabet is different, for example, Japan, China, or Saudi Arabia. The writing might look beautiful, but you have no idea how to decipher it. You may have learned to speak one of the languages in those countries but never learned how to read it. You cannot decode or connect these figures with a sound or a word. To Americans who can't read, this is everyday life. That is what English words look like to adults who speak English but can't decode the written language. Knowing that you can't read the words around you, you probably won't even really look at them or think about what they may mean.

To get an idea of what non-readers **don't** see, try this exercise: take a walk down any street in a shopping area and write down every word you see. You will be amazed by how many words surround us all the time!

Most adults who come to Literacy Chicago test somewhere between kindergarten and second-grade level readers, but they do not have the reading vocabulary to function in daily life.

Without help, they cannot:

- Read labels on a can
- Read prescription labels and instructions
- Understand signs in stores or on the street
- Buy a ticket from a machine
- Write letters, texts, or journals
- Fill out a form of any kind

- Use the internet to search for the side effects of their medications, look for a job, find out the weather, get directions, look up a movie, etc.
- Manage their money
- Write a check
- And many more.

These people are functionally illiterate.[2]

This hit home one day when one of our students won a prestigious award from the Illinois Secretary of State for his improvement in reading. Now retired, this highly intelligent 70-year-old man had had a successful career running his own company. Very smart, he managed 50 people in the glass-cutting business. However, when it came to sending checks out at the end of the month, he had to get someone to write out the amounts in words, and then he copied them onto the checks. When he retired, he decided it was time to learn three things: how to read, swim, and paint. He joined Literacy Chicago for the reading.

After he received his award from Jesse White, Illinois Secretary of State, we took him out for lunch in a Cajun restaurant. Several of us sat around the table discussing the menu and what we wanted to eat. Our student, sitting next to me, was silent. Suddenly, I realized that the menu was gibberish to him because there were many cooking terms, some of which were in French. The dishes were exquisitely described in words he had not yet learned. I quietly leaned over and helped him figure out what he wanted to eat. He proudly read his order from the menu to the waiter.

Now, when he walks down the street, he delights in reading all the words around him. He is still studying with a tutor and enjoying the challenge of increasing his vocabulary and reading at higher levels.

---

1. 1 https://nces.ed.gov/pubs2019/2019179.pdf
2. "Functional illiterate." Merriam-Webster.com Dictionary, Merriam-Webster, https://www.merriam-webster.com/dictionary/functional%20illiterate.

2

They've Got Guts

RESPECT AND ADMIRE, STARTING WITH YOUR INTAKE PROCESS.

One of the scariest actions for people who can't read is admitting out loud that they are illiterate. Many feel shame and hide this fact from family and friends. Shame, according to Brene Brown[1], means "I am bad." She explains that the antidote is empathy, which is what all adult literacy programs need to bring to people starting from intake. After shame has been articulated and responsive empathy expressed, shame does go away.

So, when an adult first contacts Literacy Chicago to tell us they need help with reading, it is a very courageous action. They are exhibiting intellectual humility, defined by Tenelle Porter, a post-doctoral researcher in the Department of Human Development at the University of California, Davis, as *"recognizing the limits of one's knowledge and valuing the insight of someone else."* Her fascinating study[2] with high school students showed that *"the more intellectually humble students were more* ***motivated to learn and more likely to use effective metacognitive strategies,*** *like quizzing themselves to check their own understanding... (She) also found that the teachers, who hadn't seen students'* *intellectual humility questionnaires, rated the more intellectually humble students as more engaged in learning."*

We respect and admire our students who have demonstrated the personal courage to come and ask for help. By letting them know that we respect them from their first contact with Literacy Chicago, we are setting them up for success. We recognize their first brave steps to improve themselves and accompany them along their path, providing caring and thoughtful training.

If you have an adult literacy program, think about this from the moment that someone dares to walk into your establishment or even call on the phone for information. They are taking the first step into the world of reading. The very first contact with someone should be encouraging and empathetic. Tell them that you recognize their courage and strength of character and that you understand how hard it is.

Explain your program to them and ensure they understand they are not alone. If you require a reading assessment, do not refer to it as a "test." Simply tell them, " We want to see where you are now so that we can measure your progress in a few months." Hopefully, your classrooms are warm and welcoming places where students feel comfortable. Your one-on-one tutoring sessions should also be based on trust, where shame is banned, and empathy is the rule. According to Brene Brown, "empathy is the cure for shame."

As your students learn to read, you will notice that they start to see themselves in a different light - in the light of a proud reader!

---

1. Brown, "Atlas of the Heart",134
2. https://behavioralscientist.org/the-benefits-of-admitting-when-you-dont-know/

3

Remember They Have Lives

DON'T MAKE QUICK JUDGMENTS

In 2018, I met the principal of a school in Georgia who was thrilled about her new online platform to connect parents and the school. It was a great idea; parents could access this website on their computers, laptops, and phones. They could get real-time updates on their children's progress, see their homework and grades, and communicate directly with the teachers. Fantastic, she thought, this will help the whole community feel more connected and involve the parents more in their kids' education.

However, it wasn't working. Many of the parents were just creating an account. "Why?" she wondered.

She sent a group of volunteers out to visit the parents in their homes and show them how to sign up and use the website. Many of the parents were uneducated, possibly illiterate, and poverty-stricken. Some of them didn't have the internet, some didn't have computers, and some didn't even have Smartphones.

However, the most heartbreaking story was about the family who was so impoverished that they could only afford one light bulb for their whole apartment. Yes, ONE light bulb that they had to move from room to room. When I heard about this, I realized that, as teachers, we have to be very mindful of our students' lives. Getting connected on this website was not high on the parents' list of priorities, and in some cases, not possible at all.

I have had numerous volunteers complain to me that the adult students they are tutoring, "forget they have a lesson," "arrive late," "don't do their HomeFun," *(we don't give home**work**)*. I always tell them that story.

All of Literacy Chicago's volunteer tutors are educated individuals who want to give back to the community and help others. It is a very noble and admirable action, much appreciated by our students. However, it is sometimes difficult to realize that the person sitting across from you may have many issues in their lives that you have never had to deal with. They have decided to improve their lives by learning to read. However, some are just getting out of prison and have to re-adapt to society; others have families who don't know they can't read so they don't want to do HomeFun in front of them. Still others have to take jobs as they come along and often work in the evenings, so they come to class or tutoring sessions without getting a full night's rest. Some have to stay home and take care of children or parents. One woman actually made herself sick worrying about an error with processing her rent that wasn't her fault. Her low level of reading made it very difficult to read the notices arriving in her mailbox. She feared that the Chicago Housing Authority would kick her out of her housing.

One of our students, who is a former drug addict, is still trying so hard to make a life for herself. She has a young child with serious health issues and no one to help her out. One day in the middle of the Covid pandemic, she called me, starving, because she had no food left in her home and nothing to feed her little girl. It is not possible, nor is it our mission for Literacy Chicago, to help our students in this way. Fortunately, and in most cases, we are able to send our students to other agencies in the Chicago area to seek such assistance. However, because it was during the Covid pandemic, our executive director, my mother, and I all put together a collection and did some grocery shopping for her.

As Karen Salmonsohn says on the website Tiny Buddha, "Please don't judge people. You don't know what it took someone to get out of bed, look and feel as presentable as possible, and face the day. You never truly know the daily struggles of others."[1]

---

1. https://tinybuddha.com/fun-and-inspiring/please-dont-judge/

4

Adults Learn Differently than Children

ANDRAGOGY INSTEAD OF PEDAGOGY

What is an "adult learner"? One of the most widely accepted definitions is Arthur Chickering's "an individual whose major role in life is something other than a full-time student."[1]

Malcolm Knowles (1913-1997) was an American educator known for the theory of andragogy (as opposed to pedagogy - the method of teaching children). Andragogy refers to principles and methods used in adult education or the art and science of helping adults learn. Knowles used this concept to document the differences between how children and adults learn. His Six Principles of Andragogy, as outlined by Kenyon and Hase (2001), citing Merriam and colleagues (2007) and Forrest and Peterson (2006), are:

- **Self-concept.** Adult learners have a self-concept. This means that they are autonomous, independent, and self directed.
- **Learning from Experience.** Adults, in particular, have the advantage of having accumulated a wealth of experiences over time. This can be a great resource for

learning as they draw upon these experiences to inform their decisions and actions moving forward.

- **Readiness to Learn.** Adults tend to gravitate towards learning subjects that matter to them. Their readiness to learn things is highly correlated with their material usefulness.
- **Immediate Applications.** The orientation of adult learning is for immediate applications rather than future uses. The learning orientation of adults tends towards being task-oriented, life-focused, and problem-centric.
- **Internally Motivated.** Adults are more motivated by internal personal factors rather than external coaxing and pressure.
- **Need to Know.** Adult learners need to know the value of what they are learning and why they need to learn the material they are asked to learn.

Let's look at the six principles defined above and compare them to how children learn.

- **Self-concept.** We know that children still need to develop their concept of who they are and what they value; they are still in the learning process.
- **Experience.** Children obviously have a short lifetime of experience, whereas adults can easily draw from their past. However, if adults have bad memories of school or difficulties learning, this can be a drawback. Children are more open to whatever they learn.
- **Readiness to Learn.** For children, going to school is their "job". They tend to take in everything at the same level of importance.
- **Immediate Applications.** Children don't worry about why they are learning something and how they might use it in the future.

- **Internally Motivated.** In most cases, children go to school because they have to; they usually don't have any personal motivation like adults do.
- **Need to Know.** Children are generally more open to learning about anything - if taught engagingly. They view the content of their lessons as valuable simply because an adult has told them that it is important. They haven't learned to discern values or what might be useful to them in the future.

Some other differences also need to be considered when working with adults. Children in educational settings can be very much alike because they often have similar socioeconomic backgrounds. Adults who come together in a group to study may have different ages, educational backgrounds, and values. One final consideration is that, in general, children learn faster than adults. Adults learn just as well, although it can take them longer!

In addition, and especially when teaching adults to read, there are many impediments to learning that are often outside their control; I will discuss these in the next Chapter.

---

1. The Office of the Illinois Secretary of State www.ilsos.gov/departments/library/literacy/oltt/adult_characteristics.html#

5

Watch out for Learning Barriers

BOTH INTERNAL AND EXTERNAL

Although Knowles's principles apply to adults in general, there are other considerations to consider when working with adults with low literacy levels. The lowest literacy rates are highly connected to poor economic mobility, health issues, and poverty. All of these factors come into play and may affect attendance, focus, and ability to learn to read.

In an article published in the Australian Journal of Adult Learning, Marina Flalasca of the Universidad Tecnológica Nacional in Buenos Aires, Argentina, divides the barriers into internal and external.

One of the internal barriers is terrible memories of school. I highly recommend not setting up your classroom to look like a traditional one. No desks in rows! Favor a circle or semi-circle where students can see each other. The classroom should have a safe, friendly atmosphere where teachers treat their adult students with respect and as equals. Teaching can be conducted more as a dialogue than as a class. The material should be at their level or slightly higher. If it is too difficult, low-literacy students tend to give up.

Teaching methodology should include auditory, visual, and kinesthetic practice. Adults who couldn't learn to read at school may be more auditory/kinesthetic learners than visual learners (See Chapter 12 - Understand Learning Styles). Think about what traditional methodology favors: writing on a board, reading rather than doing, and listening. Teachers should continually encourage all of their students' efforts and understand that different people learn differently.

Bad memories of voicing opinions in school can also be a barrier. Encouraging adult literacy students to express their thoughts and ideas is essential, even if they may not feel confident in their abilities. Creating a safe space for students to share their perspectives can empower and lead to a more fulfilling learning experience.[1]

Other internal obstructions to learning might also be their own beliefs about both ***how to learn*** and about ***new information***. Some adults might have learned that rote memorization is the only way to remember or that there are only correct and incorrect answers, with nothing in between. It is easily rejected when new information contradicts what they already know or think they know.

Fear of failure is another barrier to learning. Those students who believe they are "too old" to learn something new need to understand that the brain can continue to create new neural pathways at all ages and that challenges are actually excellent for the brain and memory. Research has demonstrated that creating learning environments containing various stimuli, such as focused attention, new experiences, and challenging activities, can promote positive improvements in brain function. While this is especially important during childhood and adolescence, enriching your surroundings can also lead to brain benefits well into adulthood.[2]

We have already alluded to external barriers to learning that are more difficult to overcome, such as poor health, poverty, and crime.

Many adult learners are older and have not always had good health care. This translates to low attendance when they have appointments with the doctor, the dentist, or at the hospital. If they have chronic illnesses, they may suffer from pain and fatigue, a condition which saps their energy and attention levels while in class.

Another external barrier that affects attendance is family issues. Women must stay home with their children because they can't afford childcare. Other family members may require the student's help at home because they also have literacy, poverty, or childcare issues.

When students are absent for an extended period, reach out and talk to them. They will appreciate the fact that you care.

Common effects of aging, such as loss of hearing and vision, may also affect their ability to be successful in class. Teachers must consider these factors by speaking louder, giving handouts with larger letters, and writing with a dark marker on a whiteboard. (Never use green markers; they are the most difficult to read.)

Poverty is also a significant factor, as in the light bulb story. We have had students who can't come to class because they couldn't afford a bus pass or just barely have enough money to eat. It is difficult for a not-for-profit organization such as Literacy Chicago to find funding to help students with their financial issues. How we would love to give out lunches or bus passes!

As teachers, we can help with overcoming some of the internal barriers to learning; sadly, the external barriers are usually beyond our control. You may not be able to solve their problems, but students will appreciate your kindness and concern.

---

1. Vemuri P, Lesnick TG, Przybelski SA, et al. Association of lifetime intellectual enrichment with cognitive decline in the older population. JAMA Neurol. 2014;71(8):1017-24. doi:10.1001/jamaneurol.2014.963
2. Vemuri P, Lesnick TG, Przybelski SA, et al. Association of lifetime intellectual enrichment with cognitive decline in the older population. JAMA Neurol. 2014;71(8):1017-24. doi:10.1001/jamaneurol.2014.963

6

Engage Adult Learners in Their Learning Process

HELP THEM HELP THEMSELVES

In Chapter 4, I discussed the difference between how adults learn versus how children learn. One of the main differences is their motivation. When adults decide to take matters into their own hands and learn to read, they have serious reasons for doing so. Some want to get jobs or better jobs. Others want to get a driver's license, pass an exam, read to their grandchildren, or simply feel more connected to the world around them.

It is essential to keep this motivation alive because it IS more challenging to learn as an adult. Learning to read as an adult is difficult, so always encourage your students. One way to do that is to get them to buy into their path to literacy. Brainstorm with your learner on things they could do independently to further their education.

Here are some ideas

- Give your learners a little notebook that they can slip into a pocket, and ask them to write down five words they see daily. You could focus on words seen in the street, at home, or in public places. At least one of the five words should be a new one. As I mentioned earlier in Chapter 1, adults with low literacy levels don't even notice the words around them. This activity will help them focus on what they can see and can read. Check their lists regularly and review past ones. You can have them write sentences or stories with the words they have noted. If necessary, use the LEA method (Chapter 27) to help them with writing.

- Take your learner to the library and ensure they have a library card. Teach them how to find books. On the first visit, help them find an appropriate book. Some libraries, such as the San Francisco public library[1], have collections of Hi-Lo books for adults. These books are high-interest books written at low levels. Avoid children's books unless they want to read them to a child. After reading that first book, encourage them to go and choose another book. You may want to accompany your learner for the first few visits.
- Create a research project with your students on a topic that interests them. Let's say that they love to cook. Have them start looking for recipes or even pictures. If they are digitally literate, show them how to google a recipe or an ingredient they particularly like. Or give them some magazines, newspapers, or a cookbook they can browse through. (All of these resources can be found at a public library.) Put all of their research into a notebook. Your student may also have their own recipes to contribute as well, which they can dictate to their tutors.
- If they have friends, family, or small children in their lives, encourage your learners to teach others to read. When their reading level gets up to third or fourth grade, they might even be able to read to children at a library or bookstore. You can help them practice the book until

they feel comfortable enough to read it with the correct pronunciation and vocal variety.

I remember the day when one of our adult learners proudly walked into my office, showing me a newspaper she had bought. She told me that now that she could read, she felt "part of the world."

---

1. https://sfpl.bibliocommons.com/list/share/380247022/711718427

7

Teaching is Personal

USE EMPATHY

Marcia Dempster, the author of *33 Ways Not to Screw Up Being a Woman in Tech,* emphasizes that building personal relationships is extremely important in business. She talks about how her favorite leaders have always been the ones who remember little details about her life and respect her with empathy.[1] When teaching adults, this dynamic is essential.

Professor John Hattie studied student-teacher relationships at the University of Melbourne[2]. He reviewed over 800 meta-analyses covering 80 million students. He concluded that those students with positive student-teacher relationships were likelier to have above-average results. He pointed out that the relationship variables that had the most influential benefits on student performance were empathy, warmth, encouragement, authenticity, and respect for their backgrounds.

Although Hattie's study was focused on schoolchildren, relationships are even more critical when working with adults. Many adults with low literacy levels had little or no support systems while growing up. There are many reasons why someone might have to face their education alone. Whatever the reason, it can be tough to go it alone sometimes. Many of their parents also had reading issues and couldn't help them; others had disabilities that were never correctly diagnosed and addressed. Some had to quit school to support their families. Sometimes, the schools they attended were overcrowded and unprepared to help struggling children. In some cultures, women are not considered eligible for education.

I am heartbroken every time I assess the reading levels of adults who graduated from high school and realize they can only read at a first or second-grade level. Others have attended school up to 8th or 9th grade with the same results. In February 2023, the Chicago Public Schools celebrated a record-high graduation rate; however, not a single student can read at grade level in 30 Illinois schools.[3]

Although we cannot go back in time to give adults the support system they missed out on, it is never too late to offer them that support. Building a positive relationship with your student can make a bigger difference in their lives than you may realize. Hattie mentions empathy as the first of the relationship variables that can provide benefits to student performance. Brene Brown[4] says: "Empathy is a tool of compassion. We can respond empathically only if we are willing to be present to someone's pain. If we're not willing to do that, it's not real empathy."

Brown explains that there is a difference between cognitive and affective empathy. The first is the ability to recognize and understand another's emotions, while the second is more about sharing one's own emotional attunement with the other's experience. She suggests that meaningful connections occur when there is a combination of compassion and cognitive empathy. How often can we really empathize with a person who may come from a completely different walk of life? Brown[5] advises, "We need to dispel the myth that **empathy** is 'walking in someone else's shoes.' Rather than walking in shoes, I need to learn how to listen to the story you tell about what it's like in your shoes *and* **believe you even when it doesn't match my experiences."**

If you can have warm, authentic, and non-judgmental conversations with your students and show them warmth and belief in their ability to learn, you will see positive effects in their lives. Another benefit for you is the joy of seeing them progress, which is what teaching is really all about!

---

1. Dempster, Marcia. (2023) 33 Ways Not to Screw Up Being a Woman in Tech. page 48.
2. Hattie, John. (2009). Visible Learning: A Synthesis of Over 800 Meta-Analyses Relating to Achievement. 10.4324/9780203887332.
3. https://wirepoints.org/not-a-single-student-can-do-math-at-grade-level-in-53-illinois-schools-for-reading-its-30-schools-wirepoints/
4. Brown, Brene (2021). Atlas of the Heart.Page 121
5. Brown, Brene (2021). Atlas of the Heart.Page 123

8

Ax or Ask?

WHEN TO TEACH MAINSTREAM ENGLISH

I borrowed this chapter's name from Dr.Garrard McClendon's fantastic book *Ax or Ask, The African American Guide to Better English.* Dr. McClendon is the renowned American professor, writer, filmmaker, and host of the PBS show *CounterPoint with Garrard McClendon.*

His book is a must-read for anyone teaching African Americans who speak Ebonics. Often called "Black English," Ebonics is not a dialect of mainstream English but a language in its own right, often referred to as African American Vernacular English (AAVE). This vernacular form of English is used for everyday communication, not for formal occasions. Ebonics was recognized as a language in 1996 when the Oakland School Board passed a resolution declaring Ebonics to be the language of 28,000 African-American students within that school district. Ebonics has its own grammatical features, vocabulary, and pronunciation.

There is nothing wrong with speaking or writing in Ebonics until a Black person uses it in a job interview or writes a professional letter. In a conversation with Dr. McClendon, he called this *linguistic discrimination.* McClendon writes*:" Discrimination has many disguises, but in America, these forms are becoming more covert...Faulty vernacular, vocabulary, articulation, enunciation, and diction can also be used to exclude certain citizens from opportunities and occupations. Black people must improve their speaking skills to avoid the pitfall of exploitation, exclusion, and economic illiteracy. Knowing the language of power and finance is gaining clout, not selling out."*

I contacted Dr. McClendon because I was pondering how to correct grammatical errors in students' writing. Reading and writing go hand in hand. Those who struggle to read also struggle to articulate their ideas on paper. When doing an exercise such as LEA (Chapter 26), we advise teachers not to correct grammatical errors. We want students to recognize their own words on the page. This seems to contradict what McClendon advocates; however, if we tell our students that in addition to not being able to read, they don't speak English properly, what effect might this have on their psychological well-being and motivation to learn to read? Imagine if you were 50 years old, and suddenly your teacher (often Caucasian) tells you that you don't speak English correctly.

So, what is the solution? On the one hand, we want to encourage our adult readers to keep coming to class and not give up when it gets tricky. On the other hand, we want to help them gain a positive self-image when interacting with those who speak mainstream English.

Dr. McClendon gave me some excellent advice. "Don't judge; just instruct!'. First of all, he suggested using the term "mainstream English" as opposed to "standard" English because the word "standard is a judgment in itself. No one, he explained, speaks "standard" English, and furthermore, he says that the average person changes dialects seven times a day. We code-switch without being aware of it when speaking to colleagues, friends, parents, teachers, or doctors. Here in the Midwest, we are lucky because the "Great Midwestern Dialect" is the dialect that news people across the country use on TV and radio. We are used to hearing and using the most mainstream English in the US.

Dr. McClendon says there are two reasons we need to express ourselves through language for two reasons. One is because we want something, and the other is because we need to be understood. To accomplish this, teachers must teach the rules of mainstream English. We need to help our students learn to read and write in what Dr. McClendon calls the "middle ground" in English, mainstream English. When doing a writing exercise such as LEA, first ensure they can read their own writing. Since written English is so different from spoken language, they may not recognize all the words they use in their daily lives.

After you are sure they can read their own words, you can teach them how to write the same thing using mainstream English. **Never say that what they wrote is wrong.** Explain that you are going to show them a **different way** to write that can be understood by anyone who reads English. Then, have them compare the two versions and let them discover the differences.

Always give students a chance to point out the differences before you give them your opinion. Let them think about it. Ask them to tell you when they would use each version of the text they composed. You and your students should have open discussions about differences and similarities. Encourage them to start thinking about code-switching and bring examples of what they hear and see to class.

Above all, be sensitive to your students' feelings and make sure they understand that you are not being judgmental in any way. You simply want them to be aware that various forms of English are used at different times and in different circumstances.

9

Classroom Environment

SAFE AND BRAVE SPACE

One of the most important things to consider when teaching a class of adult literacy learners is the environment. I am referring to both the physical setup of your classroom and the psychological aspect: the comfort level. The learners in your classroom have probably been in a classroom at some point in their lives. However, if they didn't learn to read, they probably don't have positive memories of their schoolroom environment and may not have learned appropriate classroom behavior. This is certainly true of many of our students at Literacy Chicago.

The Physical Environment

At Literacy Chicago, we strive to make the classroom as different from a traditional one as possible. Rows of chairs in which students sit facing the teacher might remind them of past unsuccessful experiences where the teacher wrote on the board, passed out handouts and books, and where learning was largely a visual experience. For those who couldn't read, this was certainly unpleasant and degrading.

You might have a fantastic lesson plan; however, if the room's layout is not conducive to learning, your learners won't enjoy it as much!

The optimal setup is a U-shape layout so that learners can make eye contact and interact. It also allows teachers to move around the inside of the U to help individual students. This space also works well for demonstrations or role plays and can create a sense of unity among the learners.

If space allows, I recommend having a few individual tables that learners can move to for break-out groups and teamwork. It is always beneficial for them to move around during a class and work with different people rather than the ones they always sit next to!

You should have good light, and the temperature should be between 65-71 degrees Fahrenheit, which is very comfortable. Keep the classroom clean and orderly, and, if possible, have the door at the back of the room so latecomers can enter without disturbing the class.

The Psychological Environment

Make sure that everyone accepts the ground rules for a successful learning environment. We talked to our learners and asked them what "rules" they thought would be appropriate. Please notice that each "rule" is written without negatives. Hang a large poster in the classroom with the rules and review them often. New students who join the class mid-term should likewise receive and sign a copy. Each of the rules came from a problem pointed out by a student!

Here is what we came up with:

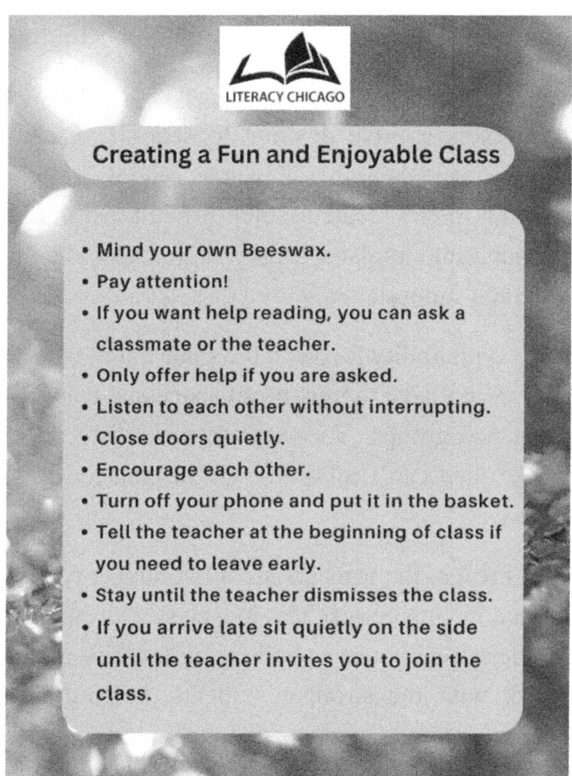

Give positive feedback! First of all, make sure you learn your students' names and that they know each other's names as well. By doing this, you acknowledge them as individuals, creating a more personal and comfortable place.

Give constructive feedback and encouragement to support your learners by explaining what they did well and then giving suggestions for improvement. Avoid using negative language and focus on the positive.

Learning to read as an adult is a huge challenge, and the fact that your learners have already decided to take it on should be applauded as often as possible. Feedback can be as simple as nodding your head, giving a "thumbs up," or smiling at your learner when (s)he performs successfully.

Encourage learners to give positive feedback to each other as well. I remember one day when a woman who was very shy and unsure of herself in class read a rather difficult text out loud. The whole class burst into applause. Just imagine how she must have felt with so much support!

If you have several ability levels in the same class, which is often the case, and if you have the luxury of space and teachers, divide the class into two groups. You want to make sure no one feels stupid because they can't follow or get disengaged because the reading is too easy.

At Literacy Chicago, the teachers are all volunteer tutors, and we have found that having co-teachers in a class addresses this situation well. Otherwise, choose a challenging text at a median level. Do pair work with the stronger students, helping the weaker ones, or give the stronger students different questions to discuss.

It is also essential to get feedback from your learners. At the end of the class, ask each person what the most important/exciting/new thing that they learned during that class was. Of course, your observation of the learners during your class will also give you an indication of how well they liked it. How engaged were they? Did they ask questions? Pay attention to their body language and facial expressions to gauge their interest.

Above all, make your classroom a comfortable place where learners can study in a positive, warm, and encouraging atmosphere.

10

What happens in Las Vegas stays in Las Vegas

CREATE A COMFORTABLE AND BRAVE ENVIRONMENT

One of the most important steps in teaching adults, whether it is reading or any other subject, is to make them feel safe. Adults who "go back to school" need to feel that they are in an environment where no one will judge them, make fun of them, or put them into an uncomfortable position. Even adults who are highly educated will sometimes hear that little voice inside of them during a meeting or a higher education course that says, "*Everyone knows more than me. I can't ask that question – they will think I am dumb.*"

Two situations where adults often feel uneasy are in ESL (or other language classes) and in basic reading classes. In language classes, there are often highly educated and successful people who are suddenly put in the position of not being able to express themselves smoothly, politely, and diplomatically and who don't understand what they hear. (They might be able to read Shakespeare, however, the spoken language is very different). This is a frustrating situation, and nearly every adult student I have met worries about looking like a fool in front of classmates.

As uncomfortable as these adults may be, it is nothing compared to how an illiterate grown-up feels the first time they walk into a classroom or even take the first step to enroll in a reading program. Adults often feel that they have failed, and it affects their whole lives.

The classroom has to be a welcoming place that doesn't look or feel like any school they attended. When a new student arrives, they should be introduced to the class in a friendly manner. I suggest having each student say their name and something about themselves. A great way to do this is to ask each person to give their name and then their favorite sport, activity, animal, movie, etc. Choose one subject, and you will see that conversation immediately begins, making the newcomer feel part of the group. The trick is setting up the situation so that everyone is on equal footing. The instructor should be more of a facilitator than a teacher. Everyone in the class needs to know that it doesn't matter if they make a mistake. Explain that no one cares. It is part of the learning process, and it is okay.

The instructor should tell the students what they will learn during the lesson at the beginning of the class and do some kind of assessment (a fill-in-the-blank, a puzzle, or a matching exercise) at the end. Hence, there is an immediate sense of accomplishment. If they go home feeling they learned something, chances are high they will return to the next class.

I also highly recommend that interactions between students are encouraged. For example, if you are having a student read a passage out loud, have the student who read call on the next student to continue. This "popcorn" technique has many benefits. Students interact with each other without the instructor having to interfere; everyone has to listen and follow along because they are not going around in a circle, and finally, if someone hasn't read, one of the others will point it out. This practice creates a group feeling. I also recommend working in small groups, which helps everyone get to know each other.

One day, I realized the importance of this when I was in my office, and a student came to talk to me in the middle of the class. When I asked her why she wasn't in class, she told me that she had just read "her page" and it wouldn't be her turn for at least another 15 minutes. To avoid this behavior, the instructor should involve the class members in every paragraph/page by ensuring that each reading passage is short enough to ask the class comprehension questions about it. The questions, too, should be asked by students, creating another interactive activity. Importantly, the instructor can also assess whether or not the class understands what they are reading.

The most important thing of all is to make sure that the students know that the classroom is like Las Vegas - whatever happens there, stays there!

11

Assessment Tools

ASSESS YOUR STUDENTS AS YOU GO!

In Steps to Teaching a Text (Chapter 21), we talk about doing learning assessments during or at the end of each class. There are important reasons to assess each lesson as you go to ensure that students have learned what you set out to teach them. Assessments, not tests!

One of the biggest reasons to have some kind of assessment is that often, adults won't ask questions when they don't understand.

So why don't adults ask these questions? Probably, because as an adult, each person feels they are the only one who does not know the answer! It's about feeling uncomfortable showing the others in the class that they aren't following.(See Chapter 10: *What happens in Las Vegas stays in Las Vegas.)*

Once, while doing a demonstration ESL class for a teaching job, I asked a student, "Do you understand?" I didn't get the job because of that question. I was told, "As a teacher, you should know whether or not your students understand!" To this day, I have never asked that question again.

That day, I learned a great lesson about teaching and ensuring that my students absorbed and comprehended the lessons. Sometimes, you can tell by the look on their face; other times, it is hard to know. So…assessments!

This should be integral to each lesson; the students don't need to know they are being assessed. Assessments are teacher tools and should be a fun part of the class. Adult students should never be singled out or embarrassed by their results if they aren't good. On the other hand, public words of encouragement are always welcome.

An excellent and amusing way to find out what students learned in a lesson is to use ***Kahoot,*** which is one of the first online platforms created for individual or team games. During a class or a one-on-one, the student sees the questions on a screen and answers on their cell phones. If you have never used it, please go ahead and give it a go. (See Chapter 31 - Resources). You can make up your own questions about your text, pop them into a game, and then play in class. When you play in team mode, students have time to discuss their answers and only put in one answer per team. You can also assign a Kahoot for HomeFun. There are also many resources on Kahoot for teachers.

Another online resource that is easy and fun is ***Quizziz*** (See Chapter 31 - Resources). This is similar to Kahoot. However, in the team mode, students play individually, but their answers all go into one team account.

With both platforms, you can review the answers with the class. It's a great way to check their actual learning.

You can easily create your own games on many more online platforms. One of our teachers came up with an idea that went over big - she created her own "Jeopardy" game as an assessment tool for each of her lessons. Students stay engaged throughout the entire lesson because they all want to win at the end! (See Chapter 33 - Resources)

If your students like crossword puzzles, you can quickly and easily create your own based on the lesson and their reading levels (See Chapter 31 - Resources). If you have a class, let the students do the puzzles individually and then check their answers with a partner. You just walk around and observe their difficulties.

An exercise to check spelling is a simple dictation. To make it more interesting, after finishing the dictation, have students ask you or their classmates questions about what they wrote. Go over difficulties together.

Another dictation exercise is to dictate questions and then have them write the answers. You can also do traditional fill-in-the-blank or matching exercises that you can create or find in pre-made lesson plans.

Interactive activities are also good for assessments. If you have a class, divide them into teams and have each team come up with a couple of critical thinking questions to try to stump the other team. (See Chapter 25 - Practice Active Reading) If you are working one-on-one, your student can ask you the questions!

The bottom line is that you need to be a little creative, keep your students on their toes, and follow up on whatever they couldn't master during the lesson.

12

Understand Learning Styles

USE ALL THREE IN EACH LESSON!

One of the biggest errors tutors make is to try to teach the way they learn. Everyone has a unique and distinct way to learn. We learn using all of our senses; however, some individuals process information based more on one sense than the others. People who rely primarily on sight are called visual learners, those who rely on hearing are auditory learners, and those who rely on touch and movement (learn by doing) are kinesthetic or tactile learners.

At the beginning of our volunteer tutor training, we ask our volunteers to take a survey to find out what their personal styles are. Here[1] is an online quiz you can answer if you want to learn more about your style.

Unsurprisingly, we have discovered that most of our volunteers are highly visual learners with a variety of auditory and kinesthetic styles. Remember, this is a person's best way to learn, not the only way. Obviously, visual learners tend to process information better through reading and writing. They like lessons based on reading a text and will often take notes during class. This is the traditional way that many schools teach, so if you are more of a visual learner, you will have an advantage.

Most of our students seem to have strong auditory and kinesthetic skills. However, some students may also have auditory processing deficits. Those students may need sentences repeated. They will also benefit from the teacher or class giving them more time to process their answer. This may explain, in part, why they struggled so much trying to learn in school.

The trick is to figure out the best way for your student to learn. Of course, we recommend using multiple styles for each lesson. However, you can focus on what is easiest for your student first. We can improve how we learn, especially if we know it. You can give the online survey to your students if you read it to them. However, if you don't want to be as formal, you can pay attention to clues revealed in their everyday activities and speech. You will get hints from what they say, "I hear what you mean.", "I see what you mean." or "That feels right." You can ask, for example: "How would you memorize a phone number without writing it down?" An auditory learner might say it a few times. A visual learner might close their eyes and "see" it, and a kinesthetic learner might want to write it in the air or use their fingers.

I remember once having an annoying (to me) ESL student who always sat next to me and repeated everything I said! It was like having a permanent echo. Guess what kind of learning style he preferred?

In the Literacy Chicago training manual, we give tips on the characteristics of learning styles and how to teach to different ones. Let me share them with you here.

Visual Learners

With pictures, the brain takes in the general image and then distinguishes details. The movement of the eyes when looking at pictures is quite different from the movement of the eyes when reading. Some students need to be taught to keep their eyes from wandering all over the page and to go from left to right when looking at words in print.

Characteristics

- Recall words after seeing them a few times
- Prefer written directions
- Can concentrate on visual tasks despite visual distractions
- Remember and understand words accompanied by pictures and graphs
- Discriminate between letters that look alike (m/n) and words that look alike (fill/full)
- Do not confuse the order of letters (spot/stop)
- Practice left-to-right or right-to-left eye movements depending on their native language.

Tutoring Strategies

- Use written instructions – not just oral ones
- Use whole language approach rather than the phonics approach
- Use pictures, charts, and graphs
- Use pictures printed on different types of paper
- TV, Radio, Film, and the Internet
- Flashcards
- Bulleted information
- Newspaper and magazine picture stories

Auditory Learners

Auditory learners learn best from techniques that employ their listening skills.

Characteristics

- Recall words after hearing them a few times
- Prefer oral instructions
- Can concentrate on listening tasks despite auditory distractions
- Use appropriate vocabulary and sentence structure
- Discriminate between words that sound alike (cat/cot) and letters that sound alike (t/d)
- Blend sounds quickly to form words
- Can retain the storyline while sounding out words

Tutoring Strategies

- Use tapes, radio, discussions, and verbal explanations
- Avoid flashcards
- Read aloud to the student
- Encourage the student to echo read (see Chapter 23 for details on echo reading)
- Encourage the student to listen to an audiobook while reading the book itself.
- Give oral instructions and not just written ones.
- Expose students to spoken words in many settings (one-on-one, recorded, radio, telephone, podcasts, and television)
- Expose the student to a variety of sounds (mechanical, animal, human, electronic, background noise)
- Use the rhythm of music to help students hear the rhythm of English phrases.

- Lecture or have them listen to a discussion
- Listen to a storyteller
- Watch a play
- Demonstrations, such as roleplaying between the tutor and the student or with other students

Tactile and Kinesthetic Learners

Some people learn best if they write down what they have heard or read in their own words to make it register in their minds. Other students need to paraphrase aloud what they have heard or read. These tactile and kinesthetic learners learn best by using body movements and the sensations those body movements produce.

Characteristics

- Recall words after writing them a few times
- Move smoothly, rhythmically, and freely
- Recall words more easily when walking or pacing
- Remember the feeling of a story better than the details
- Recall words after typing them a few times
- Excel at crafts such as sewing or making models
- Write legibly and proportionately
- Recall words after touching the object they represent or using them in a game.

Strategies

- Use Scrabble tiles, alphabet cutouts, or lettered dice to make words
- Play games that let the student identify the answer by manipulating something concrete rather than just speaking the answer out loud

- Use computers and experience stories as learning tools
- Take notes
- Make models
- Have the student make their own flashcards
- Use alphabet cut-outs made of wood, sandpaper, or textured materials for spelling practice.

Knowing your own learning style has many benefits besides being aware of how you teach someone something. After discovering that I am a kinesthetic/visual learner with low levels of auditory memory, I realized why I was having so much difficulty working with a colleague. When I had a message for her or asked her to do something for me, I always followed up with an email or handed her the message I had written down. She would say, " You already told me, why are you doing this?" She took my written notes as an insult to her competence. On the other hand, when she told me something, and I didn't write it down, she would get upset when I asked her again. "I told you yesterday. Why are you bugging me again?"

I quickly learned to write down everything she told me and not to bother leaving her notes!

---

1. https://www.learningstylequiz.com/

13

HomeFun instead of Homework

WHO WANTS TO WORK?

As soon as a teacher says the word "homework," most people think of something they have to do, not something exciting that they want to do. How many times have parents said to their kids," Have you done your homework?" only to be answered with grunts and complaints?

For the last ten years or so, I have been trying to change from the idea of "WORK to do" at home to something enjoyable and FUN! Most of my students have embraced the idea and, surprisingly, are more apt to do their assignments promptly and enthusiastically. Science has shown that emotional events, especially pleasurable ones, are always easier to remember. Dr. David Linden has written extensively about this concept in his book *The Compass of Pleasure (Viking, 2011).* When we experience any type of pleasure (including drugs, sex, exercise, and altruistic actions.), the brain creates the neurotransmitter dopamine. This is then absorbed by neurons in other parts of the brain, creating new neural pathways and helping to cement the memory of that pleasurable feeling.

Fun and engaging activities produce this dopamine, thus allowing students to anticipate doing more assignments instead of being grumpy about their "work."

Most adults who decide to join a reading class are already doing something a little bit out of their comfort zone. In addition, most of them have negative feelings about school because they couldn't succeed there. Just mentioning the word "homework" motivates them to pack up their notebooks and stop listening.

HomeFun is the solution to encourage students to continue engaging in their reading experience outside of class and make them more aware of the written words around them. Think about including assignments that focus on sight words and other words they need in their daily lives.

Here are a few ideas:

- Write down words they see in the street on their way home.
- Write down words on a list of ingredients on a can or microwaveable package in their home.
- Copy the names of signs listed in the aisles of their neighborhood supermarket or department store.
- Look at labels on their clothes to find washing instructions.
- Give them a little notebook to write new words they see outside of class - I suggest having them find five words each day. You will be surprised to see how many more they will bring you!
- Give crossword puzzles and word games to do based on the new words learned in the lesson.
- Bring a shopping list to class.
- Write a list of errands, and bring it to class.
- Make a list of words they see on public transportation.

- Circle all the words they recognize on a piece of mail they receive (advertisements, etc.)
- Assign Kahoot and Quizziz for them to do on their phones.
- Write a list of rhyming words that are spelled the same way. For example, how many words rhyme with "meet"? (feat and meat don't count! Beet does.)

You can make some of these assignments into competitions, with the person bringing the longest list being the winner. Or you can create teams where everyone works alone but combines their lists in class.

Once they bring back their HomeFun, be creative in the way you exploit it in class. Each person can share their lists with the rest of the class. You can ask everyone to get up and write their lists on the board, and then the students have to read each other's lists out loud. Or one person can "dictate" their list to the whole class or a partner. In addition, when students " teach" the words, they will feel good about themselves. They go from being the student who always fails to being the successful teacher!

The more imaginative you are, the more your students will enjoy the experience.

14

Use Adult Material

CHILDREN'S BOOKS ARE FOR CHILDREN!

If you are teaching adults to read or training volunteers on how to teach reading to adults, be sure to use adult reading materials and most definitely NOT children's books. New instructors often choose children's books because they are not aware of other sources of low-level reading materials.

It is extremely demeaning to give a children's book to an adult just because it is at their reading level. I have had countless arguments over the use of children's books in the context of usefulness vs. demeaning activity. Volunteer tutors may argue that these children's stories teach many lessons, such as accepting others even if they are not like you or keeping your promises. Tutors say that students enjoy reading books for kids because they are relatively easy. There are plenty of interesting things for adults to read without making them feel they can only read baby stories!

There are several collections of leveled books for adults, which are called ***Hi-Lo*** books.[1] These are books that have high-interest levels and low-level readability. In addition to focusing on the basic vocabulary, the best of these books:

- Have a punchy or fun style while using shorter words and sentences.
- Are age appropriate.
- Are fun to read aloud.
- Have straightforward storylines without too many flashbacks or sophisticated storytelling devices that might be hard for a struggling reader to understand.
- Aren't too long.

When a student can read and understand an entire book, their self-confidence is boosted immensely, and they will soon be asking for more!

While I usually stick to my guns about using adult material for adults, there are a few exceptions in which using children's materials is useful. One is if a student **specifically asks** to read a children's book. For example, your student has children or grandchildren and wants to read to them. Then, this is the adult student's ***choice*** and meets their specific goals and objectives.

Often, children and grandchildren aren't aware that their elders don't know how to read. Kids who see their parents or grandparents struggling to learn how to read a children's book realize just how important it is to take advantage of their own schooling.

Another exception is in the use of material that is written for children in school. There are many excellent websites, such as Read Works, that have lesson plans for levels K through 12. You will be surprised to see how sophisticated some of them can be, especially those about history, geography, and art.

---

1. Check Chapter 33 for a list of publishers that specialize in hi/lo readers.

15

Teach Interesting Content

IT'S STIMULATING TO LEARN NEW THINGS!

When I first joined Literacy Chicago, we had several classes to teach reading. I visited all the classes and learned a lot about different methods used by the volunteer teachers. After much observation of the students' engagement, I realized that students were more involved when the subject matter was something that they could relate to. In addition, they were fascinated by many different topics.

I became aware of the fact that, even if they had gone to school, they hadn't been able to take advantage of what was being taught because of their reading issues. (Think about all the things you learned in grade school while you were learning to read). They know there are many subjects they haven't had a chance to learn. Reading lessons that also teach something beyond simply sounding out words keep students interested and feed their hunger for knowledge.

If you manage the curriculum for an organization with several classes, then make sure each class has its own theme so that tutors don't choose the same material. You don't want every class to do readings on a holiday just because it is coming up. In our organization, that would be eight readings on the same thing during a week. Students will get disengaged.

Here are a few ideas that have been successful at Literacy Chicago:

- "Reading for Everyday Life". Students learn to do things such as filling out forms, reading maps, or going grocery shopping.
- "Reading the World" gets into science, geography, and the world around us. Students have been fascinated with their texts on animals, and often one can hear loud debates about subjects such as the relationship between horses and zebras!
- "American Trivia" delves into interesting facts, figures, and people from American history. The class ends with an online version of the game "Jeopardy."
- "Learn to Read Through Theater" teaches students how to "see" what they read and then interpret their ideas on how it should be read.
- "Phonics Fun" is a basic 12-week phonics course that includes American blues and folk songs that focus on the particular phonics being taught, and incorporates online games such as Kahoot and the use of Google Jamboards.*
- "Tell your Story" teaches students how to organize their ideas and tell, then write, their own stories with a beginning, middle and end.

A few words about storytelling. You might get some resistance to storytelling because your student may have difficulties putting together a coherent story. However, teaching storytelling encourages active participation in class, enhances students' communication skills, and fosters their imagination. It makes them think about using rich vocabulary to enhance their stories and engage their readers. Suddenly, the tables are turned, and others are reading their work. What a great way to build self-confidence!

Be creative, and whether you are teaching a group or doing one one-on-one tutoring, the secret is to find what makes your student tick and find activities around it.

16

Letting Down Your Hair

BEING SILLY IN A NON-TRADITIONAL LEARNING ENVIRONMENT

I used to call this "being silly"; however, during recent in-service training for my volunteer team, I found out that the word "silly" means different things to different people, such as foolish, stupid, or unintelligent. So, taking the suggestion of one of the participants, let's call this action "letting down your hair." The concept is to get as far away from a traditional style class as possible.

Remember that an adult who can't read may have gone to school, but they certainly didn't succeed in learning the way they were taught. The solution is to find new and fun ways to engage students by allowing them to relax completely and enjoy themselves. When I began teaching ESL in the 70s in Orleans, France, I quickly realized that students remembered more when they were having fun. Ever since then, I have included very non-traditional teaching methods and exercises during which people could laugh and really "let down their hair." After a group of people has engaged in a "silly" activity together, something happens. They realize that whatever errors they may make, they won't be sillier than they have been in a group.

I remember once when I was a very young and inexperienced teacher. I had a group of very distinguished members of the community in my class. There were several doctors, including the head of the largest hospital in the city, a psychiatrist, and a dermatologist. Other students were elected members of the municipal council. Although they were serious about learning English, they were also ready to engage in what I call "silly" fun. For example, during one class, I actually had them holding hands and singing children's songs such as "The Farmer in the Dell" and "London Bridge." I am ready to wager that they still know the names of all the animals on the farm AND the way they "talk" in English!

Applied psychologist Aditya Shukla, writes about why fun and engagement improve learning. He writes on the website Cognition Today: *"Research shows that having fun while learning avails unique cognitive resources, associates reward and pleasure with information strengthens and broadens memory networks, and toggles between 2 basic neural modes – one for diffused mind-wandering and the other for focused attention."* [1]

Our adult literacy students have joyfully participated in games such as "Simon Says", and "Hangman", singing funny songs, drawing and then writing about ridiculous pictures, as well as playing a variation of charades where the students write a word and the others have to act it out.

Here are some more ways Aditya Shukla suggests you can incorporate fun into your lessons:

- *Use the SHoP rule   Surprise, Humor, and Play*
- *Make the environment conducive to social interactions*
- *Engage in simple physical activities like asking students to do something trivial*
- *Use pop culture references*

- *Connect real-life moments to fictional lecture moments*
- *Exaggerate points, add a dramatic flair*
- *Mix emotions and transition between high intensity, curiosity, neutral, and mike-drop moments. Transitions are important; keeping a single emotion on for too long won't help much*
- *Use props & games*
- *Develop a persona to play with student and teacher expectations & a unique style to build familiarity.*
- *Use memes*
- *Develop relationships*

So let your hair down and have some fun with your students. Not only will they enjoy it, it will be very beneficial for their learning experience.

---

1. https://cognitiontoday.com/why-fun-improves-learning-mood-senses-neurons-arousal-cognition/

17

Teacher Stand Back

MAKE THE CLASS STUDENT-FOCUSED

Carol Bausor,[1] a successful conference speaker, coach, consultant, and teacher-trainer in the academic and corporate world, gave me some of the best advice I have ever received as a teacher. It is the concept of what I call "teacher stand back." I don't remember what Carol called it when I worked under her expert leadership at a language school in Paris. At the time, I was managing a group of about 100 language teachers from around the world, developing curricula, and teaching high-level classes.

During the first training that Carol gave all of the teachers when she took over the role of Program Director, she divided all of us into groups and gave us tasks to do. Each task lasted about 15 minutes. After we had finished, she asked us to tell her what SHE had been doing. Nobody knew. We were all so engaged in our own learning experience that we forgot about her.

Carol had, in fact, been sitting quietly on the side of the class doing - nothing! This is the secret to keeping your energy levels up, she explained. It is important for teachers to stand back and chill while allowing students to learn by themselves. Any teacher knows how tiring it is to be dynamic, interesting, and captivating for hours at a time. So, this is a time to observe - and relax. In addition, when teaching adults to read, this approach gives the students more responsibility for their own learning.

So, how do you accomplish relaxing and standing back during your class? Let's look at a few scenarios.

Introducing a New Text

Let's say you have a text on zebras. How often do you think your students think about zebras? Probably not every day. In fact, they might not know much about them at all. Remember, since they can't read, they missed out on many basic facts about the world around us because they couldn't keep up in school.

Before even handing them the text, you need to create some excitement and interest. One way is to simply give them a few facts about zebras (boring!) You could either ask the whole class to tell you what they know (Know-Want-Learn) and make notes on the board, OR you could put them in pairs or groups and ask them to discuss the subject and then report back to the group. Be sure to guide them by asking a couple of questions before they go into groups, such as, "Do you think zebras are in the same family as horses? What do zebras look like? Where do they live? What do they eat? How fast can they run?"

Give the groups a few minutes to come up with their ideas, and then, as a whole class, discuss the results. While they are working together, YOU sit and relax!

Having done this exercise once with a group of students at Literacy Chicago, I can assure you that they had various and very strong ideas about this relatively obscure (to them) subject.

Making Them the "Teacher"

Another way to "stand back" is to let them ask each other questions. Let's say you read the first paragraph of the text to them. You then say, "Krystil, please ask someone else a question about what I just read." She chooses a student who then answers - or can ask for "help" from another classmate. That student then asks a question to another student. What are you doing? Standing back.

Correcting Each Other's Work

If you are teaching students to recognize specific sounds or sight words, divide students into groups and assign a paragraph to each group after studying the text. Instruct them what to look for (all the 'on' and 'an' sounds, for example). Each group makes a list and then writes it on the board. Then, THEY check each other's lists. (You stand back and watch). Make sure though, that you do this in groups. When individuals try to "help" each other by correcting them, some students take it very emotionally because they need a little more time to think.

With a little thought, you, as a teacher, can find many ways for your students to engage while you are recharging your batteries!

---

1. https://www.linkedin.com/in/carol-bausor-562b603/

18

Sight Words

WHAT ARE THEY ANYWAY?

Sight words are words that a person can read on sight. They are also called high-frequency words because they often appear in the English language. They occur so often that it makes more sense to memorize them rather than trying to sound them out each time you see them (as may be done with other, less common words). Some examples of sight words include "the," "and," “has,” “was,” and "they."

In a way, sight words are like a secret handshake between readers and writers. When you're reading, being able to recognize a word without sounding it out is like getting a nod from someone familiar with what you're doing - it's reassuring and helps you to focus on understanding what you're reading rather than having to stop every few seconds to figure out how to pronounce a word so that they know what it means.

The other side of that equation is that when you're writing something down, you are using sight words. The reader will then be able to recognize the word immediately; they won't have to stop and sound it out, so they'll understand your message much quicker!

Sight words can be divided into four groups:

- Survival: words that need to be recognized for day-to-day life. These words may be related to safety, jobs, emergencies, or consumers. Some examples are poison, post office, ladies or men's room, sale, stop, walk, don't, open, and closed.
- Service or utility: words that appear frequently. They can also be abstract words that do not have meaning alone but are needed to understand an idea, such as a, and, the, who, what, where, when, etc.
- Irregularly spelled: words such as have, women, tough, telephone.
- Rhyming: words that rhyme and are spelled the same way, such as hat, cat, bat, and pat.

Edward Williams Dolch published one of the most common lists of sight words in 1936. This list contains 220 words made up of conjunctions, prepositions, pronouns, adverbs, adjectives, and verbs. He was an advocate of the "whole word reading approach" and "argued that his list was used in 75% of all school texts, libraries, newspapers, and magazines."[1]

Although he didn't include any nouns in his list, Dolch did create a list of nouns for children learning to read. I suggest that you teach your students the nouns they need in their daily lives.

Why are sight words so important for adults?

The obvious benefit of learning your sight words is that your students will be able to read a lot faster. Because they'll quickly recognize all of those familiar, high-frequency words, they won't have to stop and try to sound them out each time they come up. This will help them breeze through their reading material and increase confidence.

There's another benefit: learning sight words will help strengthen the connection between sounds and letters. This connection is especially helpful for English learners because English has an irregular spelling system. In the next chapter, I will discuss how you can take "sight word breaks" to help students see and hear the connections.

---

1. https://adayinourshoes.com/dolch-sight-words/

19

Teach Sight Words in Context

READING WORDS THAT MATTER

Reading is fun, but learning to read can be difficult. So how do you motivate people who aren't familiar with reading to love it? One way is to teach them **sight words;** however, be sure to teach them in context.

One of the biggest challenges for adult literacy tutors is finding ways to teach them that make it easy and fun for their students. This can be especially difficult if the tutor has a very different background from their student. For example, a young man who loves video games might struggle to figure out how to teach a middle-aged woman who can't quite get the hang of technology and is interested in cooking. A lot of teachers give students random lists of sight words to memorize, however, this is not very exciting or helpful. In fact, it can even put students off on reading, because they don't know what to do with all of these lists.

So, let's go back to the woman who loves cooking and wants to be able to read a recipe. Simply giving her a list of ingredients to memorize would be pretty tough. Instead, if the tutor had a recipe that showed pictures of the ingredients, it would be so much easier to make the connection between the word and the image. A study published in 2015 shows that when adults read, a specialized brain area actually recognizes printed words as pictures rather than by their meaning.[1]

That's why flashcards with sight words (especially nouns) have little pictures on them so that when they see the word, they can remember what it looks like and what it means — even if it's a hard word to pronounce.

It's easy for adults to forget the words they have learned, so make sure your student has a strategy that works for them. This list of ideas will help make sure they'll remember their sight words after they learn them.

Search in their own writings: after having your student write a short text, look at the words together, and ask them to point out the ones they recognize. Then, brainstorm with them to find similar words. For example, if they write " furry," you can teach them the pattern of **Consonant, Consonant +Y**. Ask them what other words they can come up with ("funny," "sunny," "tummy," and "finally.")

Create a list by interest (around the house, to-do, shopping..) Help them write a shopping list, for example, then go on a field trip to the grocery store where they can find the items on their list. These are the words that are important to them.

Students create their own flash cards. Give each student a pack of index cards where they can write new words. You might ask them to write a sentence on the other side of the card using the word or draw a picture to help them remember. Encourage them to find other words that match, such as rhyming words that are spelled the same way, and note them on the card as well.

Look through magazines or newspapers to recognize words. Bring in a magazine or text and ask them to circle all the words they already know before starting to read. After they have scanned the text and circled all the words they already know, plus the "a", "the," and other service words, they can focus on the more difficult ones. It won't seem as daunting if many words in the text have already been circled!

Teach words in context (street signs, menus, etc.). Take your student for a walk outside and have them write down all the words they see. Go to a store and do the same thing. Take a trip to a museum or a zoo and read the signs at the exhibits. Be sure to follow up on all the new words at your next tutoring session or class.

Take "sight word breaks." While working on a text, stop if you notice a word with a certain pattern and have your student search for more words with the same pattern. For example, you see the word "hat". Ask them to tell you all the words that rhyme with it, such as bat, fat, and sat. Make sure you are teaching patterns. If the word is "flake," for example, and the student says "steak" (that you eat), this is a good teaching moment. Simply explain that "steak" does not fit the written pattern, although it is pronounced the same way, and that English is sometimes very confusing!

---

1. https://www.scientificamerican.com/article/when-we-read-we-recognize-words-as-pictures-and-hear-them-spoken-aloud/

20

Reading Out Loud

IMPROVES MEMORY AND COMPREHENSION

Nearly all adult literacy students need to read aloud before they can read silently. Most of them love to do so. However, you must set them up for success before letting them read, especially for beginners or very low-level readers.

I remember once, while observing classes, I saw a teacher assign a reading passage to one of the students. This student was asked to read an entire page. She stumbled through it, and the teacher quickly corrected her each time she had a problem. When she (finally) finished, the teacher simply asked the next student to read and proceeded to go around the table student by student. What is wrong with this scenario? Everything! First of all, the teacher did not allow the student to figure it out for herself; secondly, the passage was way too long; thirdly, the teacher didn't ask any comprehension questions; and finally - all the other students were bored, couldn't follow her slow pace, and some were even drifting off to sleep. Is this reading? I equate this to simply sounding out words as you might do with a foreign language. You might be able to pronounce all the words on a list;

however, you can't possibly understand the meaning if you don't know the language.

Many studies show benefits to reading out loud, such as improving memory and increasing comprehension. Researcher Colin Macleod, a psychologist at the University of Waterloo in Canada, studied the impact of reading out loud on memory. He found that people consistently remember words and texts better when they read aloud. His studies have been replicated numerous times, and in one study, adults aged 67 to 88 were asked to read words silently and then aloud. They could remember 27% of the words read aloud and only 10% of the words they read silently.[1]

The way to handle reading aloud differs depending on whether you are working with a student one-on-one or in a class setting. However, some overall strategies will help in all cases. First of all, never ask a low-level adult literacy student to read a text "cold." (See Chapter 21, "Steps to Teaching a Text") Reading out loud is the very LAST step after they have studied and understood it.

Many students tend to look at the first letters of the word and anticipate the rest. So, for example, the word "father" might become faith or fast. Articles, prepositions, and word endings (-s, -ed -ing) are often either added in or simply overlooked. Make sure you don't let these errors go uncorrected, and teach your students to look carefully at the whole word - all the way to the end. Let them try to correct themselves and only give them the proper pronunciation if they can't. Encourage them each time they get it with a big YES!, a nod of your head, or a thumbs up!

In addition, although punctuation may be second nature to you, students are often confused by what they call "those little dots" or "those squiggly lines." Make sure they understand that a period is the end of a sentence. In addition, teach them that punctuation influences how we use our voices—for example, dropping your voice at the end of a declarative sentence or raising it when there is a question mark. It can be fun for students to read a sentence with big excitement when their attention is drawn to the exclamation point at the end.

If you are working one-on-one, you can let them take all the time they need to sound out words. You can work intensely on their pronunciation and inflection. Fight the urge to correct them and let them work it out until they can complete the word.

However, if you are in a group setting, it is a bit different. The adults in your group may be at different reading levels. In classes at Literacy Chicago, there is a mix of students who can barely read in the same class as those who are just past the 4th-grade level. It is essential to give everyone a chance to read and keep everyone engaged.

Here are a few tips:

- Instead of just going around in a circle, you choose the next reader to keep students on their toes.
- If everyone in the group is at the same level, have them choose the next reader.
- When you choose the readers, give longer and more complex passages to higher-level students. Focus more on their inflection and pronunciation so the meaning is clear.
- After a student reads, allow them to ask a question about what they read to someone in the group. This ensures that both the reader and the listeners understand the texts.
- At the end of a paragraph or a thought, stop and ask a couple of comprehension questions to check for understanding. Even if you have followed all of the steps in teaching a text, you might find that some people

still haven't comprehended everything. ***Remember that adults are often embarrassed to ask questions if they think everyone else understands except for them!***

- If there is a dialogue in the text, divide it among your students, encouraging them to read as if they were the person in the story.

Remember always to encourage them and never hesitate to have them read the same passage repeatedly until they can do it smoothly. This practice will inspire, motivate, and give them confidence. Their HomeFun can simply be practicing reading out loud.

---

1. https://www.bbc.com/future/article/20200917-the-surprising-power-of-reading-aloud

21

Steps to Teaching a Text

FROM CHOOSING THE TEXT TO READING OUT LOUD

Follow the steps listed below when you are teaching a text to ensure comprehension, engagement, and the joy of reading!

1. There are three criteria to consider when you choose a text for your student(s) to read:

- **Reading Levels** - Give students a text just a little bit above their current level to challenge them while not making it overwhelming.
- **Think about your students' interests** - not yours! Just because you are passionate about politics doesn't mean your students have the background to understand election results. Remember that if your student can't read, it probably means they haven't succeeded in school, so they lost out on a lot of learning possibilities. Find something they are passionate about to engage their interest.
- **Length** - Assigning *Moby Dick* would be discouraging to your students as soon as they see how many pages are in the book. Start with shorter texts that you can read in

a session. They will gain confidence from completing the entire text. An excellent site to find short and interesting texts is Read Works. (See Chapter 33 - Resources)

2. Before reading the text, pre-teach using "Know-Want-Learn + Vocabulary (see Chapter 22 for instructions)

3. Read the entire text out loud to give students an overview.

- Since your students are fluent English speakers, they will understand the text when you read it to them.
- Tell them to follow along by using their finger as you read it out loud.
- Some students might just like to listen, which is fine. Many adult literacy students are auditory learners, so this is a good way for them to grasp the general meaning of what they are about to read.

4. Divide into paragraphs
Read each paragraph in the following manner:

- Choose and list several vocabulary words to study before reading.
- Start by practicing echo reading (Chapter 23) and then duet reading (Chapter 24), and then discuss the ideas
- **Do a short assessment exercise** (Chapter 11)
- Let students read out loud in a group or one by one

5. Reading the whole text out loud in a class setting

- Let students read aloud one by one. (Chapter 20)

6. Assess their learning

- To check that everyone has understood the lesson, do an assessment. It can be a fill-in-the-blank, a word puzzle, a matching exercise, a crossword puzzle, or a Kahoot! The more creative you are, the more fun your students will have. You can make this into a group competition or have them do it individually.

Summing up

- Finally, ask them if they learned what they wanted to learn about the subject (Know-Want-Learn), and what else they learned. If they are still curious about the subject and want to learn more about it, consider choosing another reading about the same thing!

22

Use KWL +V

ENGAGE INTEREST BEFORE READING

KWL stands for Know-Want-Learn. This is a method to stimulate a student's interest in a subject. Once you have captured their attention, they will be eager to learn. Always find out what people know about a subject before you start "teaching" it. This goes for anything you teach. I discovered early in my teaching days that by asking questions to find out what students already knew and then what they wanted to know, I could hold their attention. In this way, they would have fun learning almost anything, including difficult points of grammar.

I believe that KWL is one of the very best ways to teach any subject to adults learning to read. Let me explain exactly how it works and what I have added to it!

Let's say you are going to give them a short text to read about penguins. Now, most adults don't spend much time thinking about these fascinating birds. Most people haven't even seen one except on TV or at a zoo or aquarium. So, start by asking them what they know about penguins. To make it more fun, you might even show a short funny video. **Always remember that**

although your students know how to speak English, they may not know what it looks like in its written form.

Students brainstorm together, and in the course of describing what they know, if they happen to say any of the words with irregular spellings or any of the words that are in your text, you note it in a **vocabulary list** on the board. (*That is my personal addition to the KWL+ V*).

You also make a list of what they "know" on the board without correcting them. So, if they tell you that penguins live in the northern half of the earth, and you know that the text says they live in the southern hemisphere, you still write it on your chart. Now that you are talking about penguins, ask students what they "want" to know about them, and add it to the chart.

You still aren't quite ready to read the text. Pull out the difficult vocabulary words, and go over them with students. Then, give them the text, and have them circle those words. Finally, read and discuss it using the methods explained in **Chapters 23 and 24.**

When you finish reading, come back to your chart. Ask students to tell you what they have learned. Discuss differences between what they "knew" and the information in the reading.

KNOW	WANT	LEARN	VOCABULARY
Penguins live in the northern half of the earth	*What do penguins eat?* *Do they fall in love?* *How do they communicate?* *Do they have feathers?* *Can they fly?*	*Penguins are emotional.* *Penguins stay with the same mate.* *Penguins can't fly but they have feathers.* *Penguins live in the southern half of the earth.*	*Penguin* *Feather* *Love* *Food*

Penguins was actually the subject of a class recently, and at the end, students were excitedly telling me what they had learned. Who would have thought that a group of adult students from Chicago would have gotten so enthusiastic about these birds?

I owe it to our amazing tutor, Karen Fredrickson, and of course, the simple and useful KWL+V!

23

Echo Reading

REPEATING WHAT STUDENTS HEAR AND SEE

Echo reading is what you might think it is - the teacher reads a sentence or a long phrase, and the student repeats it. This strategy, albeit simple, has many advantages for adults learning to read and can also be used for beginner ESL students.

First, students need to hear how fluent reading sounds. "It shouldn't be a surprise to learn that students must hear fluent readers begin modeling if they are to understand how they should sound when they read fluently." (Miller and Veatch, 2011).[1] When painfully sounding out word after word in a sentence, an adult learner focuses on saying each syllable separately. They often don't know what they are reading. Using this technique allows learners to hear and understand the sentence before reading it aloud. This helps with comprehension, fluency, and pronunciation.

For echo reading to be effective, learners must follow along the page with their fingers as the teacher reads aloud, and again when they repeat. Although experienced English language readers automatically read from left to right, adults learning to read need to train their eyes to do just that. Following along with their finger also helps them to see every word in the text. "There's an emphasis that the strategy is much more complex than it appears to be. Research has shown that matching speech to print is an underlying skill of a specific word learning" (Jennings, Caldwell, and Lerner, 2014)[2]

This technique works equally well when teaching ESL students. The main difference is that adults who speak English and are learning to read will understand more quickly, whereas ESL students might not know the vocabulary. I recommend pre-teaching the vocabulary to ESL students before you start echo reading.

In Chapter 21 - Steps to Teaching a Text echo reading for adult learners comes after discussing the subject of the text, reading it aloud to them once, and going through the "Know and Want" parts of Know-Want Learn (Chapter 22)

I recommend having fun with this strategy. When you read to your students, emphasize keywords, read at a normal speed, and naturally use inflection. Then LISTEN to your learners; if they are not echoing you precisely the way you want them to, repeat the sentence until they get it right. They will experience a lot of satisfaction in reading the way you do. It is also a good idea to stop and check comprehension of difficult words or ideas.

Some ways to make echo reading more interesting and fun:

- If you are working with a group of students, you might want to divide the class into two groups and have them alternate echo reading.
- Make it a competition to see which group is doing better
- If they aren't speaking loudly enough, have them stand up.
- If you have a stronger student in the group, ask them to read the echo reading.

- Be sure to make echo reading an enjoyable and amusing activity!

After echo reading, you can go on to the next step: duet reading! (Chapter 24)[3]

---

1. Miller, M., & Veatch, N. (2011). Literacy in Context (LinC): Choosing Instructional Strategies to Teach Reading in Content Areas for Students Grades 5-12. Pearson.
2. Jennings, J., Caldwell, J., & Lerner, J. (2014). *Reading problems assessment and teaching strategies.* Boston, MA: Pearson Education, Inc.
3. For more information and ideas on Echo Reading: Echo Reading - STRATEGIES https://strategiesforspecialinterventions.weebly.com/echo-reading.html

24

Duet Reading

READING TOGETHER

When I was an ESL teacher I thought I had invented the method of having students read out loud with me. Later, I learned that ***the Illinois Secretary of State recommends duet reading*** in their Volunteer Tutor Training manual. This is another tried and true method to enhance comprehension and fluency. You simply ask the students to read along with you, mimicking the intonation, rhythm, and stress of each line. It is highly effective.

First, select reading material that is of interest to the student. (This is essential.) It can be a little bit above their comfort zone; however, if it is too difficult they may become discouraged. You start reading with expression at a **normal speed** and instruct your students to use their fingers to follow along in the text. This is very important because adult beginners have not learned to follow a text from left to right. Our students often get lost because their eyes just don't know which way to go as someone is reading to them.

Keep going even if your student can't keep up. If your student gives up, take a brief pause and ask them if it's ok to continue.

Repeat this process several times in different ways. If you are working with a group of students, break them up into teams and have them read along with you by team. Alternate between teams as you read the text. Make it into a game encouraging "teams" to read louder than the others. Adults love competition, especially if it is on a team. Make sure you set up your teams so that you have a mix of stronger and weaker students on each one. This allows the weaker students to be included without feeling overwhelmed or embarrassed.

If you have students whose reading levels are higher than the others, assign them as team captains. Let them lead the duet reading for their respective teams.

At the end, you declare it a tie!!

Although the conventional utilization version of duet reading instructs to avoid asking comprehension questions, I believe that it is of the utmost importance to do so. What is the point of reading if you don't understand?

To see how it feels to read without comprehension, try reading aloud from a text written in another language that you don't know but which uses the same alphabet, but that you don't know. It's just a bunch of gibberish.

Choosing the right material for duet reading is key. You want something short and simple enough for students to follow easily. Some material written for beginning ESL students is appropriate. In my ESL classes, I often used either poetry or Caroline Graham's *Jazz Chants*[1], which she says is, "just spoken American English with an awareness of the natural rhythms." She has written several books of chants using simple, down-to-earth vocabulary. They are often very amusing, short, and easy to understand.

A young woman joined Literacy Chicago's adult reading classes, and I assigned her a tutor. After a few weeks, the tutor called me in desperation, because his student was having so much trouble reading anything he gave her. I suggested trying out the *Jazz Chants**. Miracle! He reported back to me that not only did she love them, but her reading levels have started to improve steadily. She has gained confidence and joins in during all of our classes, even if she can't always keep up.

Duet Reading can be followed by Shadow Reading, which is a similar technique. The teacher and student read together; however, the teacher's voice fades in and out, letting the student continue alone. As the student becomes more proficient, the teacher speaks more softly, gradually becoming silent, allowing the student to read on their own.

So, look for fun material and enjoy duet reading with your students!

---

1. Find an online version of *Small Talk : More Jazz Chants,* Carolyn Graham' in Chapter 33 - Resources

25

Practice Active Reading

FOCUS ON COMPREHENSION AND CRITICAL THINKING QUESTIONS.

Have you ever found yourself so immersed in a book that you forget everything else? You are in another world, with all the smells, sounds, feelings, and scenes that may be foreign to your daily life. While you are reading, your mind is highly active: predicting, making connections, contextualizing, critiquing, adding new information to your personal database, and thinking of how to use it. You might even fall into the temptation of looking at the last page because you just NEED to know how it ends…

Your brain is also making all kinds of connections, your left frontal lobe is activated to decipher letters and words, your anterior temporal lobe is busy analyzing word flow and their tenses, and your limbic system (a set of brain structures that support emotional, behavioral, and memory functions) is busy triggering emotions that help you accept and remember information.

This is called "Active Reading," and you are, consciously or unconsciously, evaluating, second-guessing, summarizing, anticipating, inferring, strengthening your comprehension, and interacting with the text you are reading.

Your goal for your students should be to bring them to this level of understanding and enjoyment of the written word.

Here is how you can practice Active Reading with your students:

Before Reading:

- Engage them! First, before reading, be sure to preview the vocabulary. Have a look at titles, subtitles, pictures, charts, and graphs. Ask your students to predict what might happen. Go over any vocabulary words that might be unfamiliar or difficult to understand. Incite them to think about what kind of text this might be. Is it funny? Factual? Imaginary? A story? A poem? Look back at Chapter 22 (KWL) for more ideas about conversations before reading.
- You might give them a "mission". Ask a few questions that they need to find the answers to in the text. Underline, circle, or highlight the responses.
- Make it a "word scavenger hunt" where they identify words and must use each word in a sentence of their own. Create teams for this. Have a small prize for the winner(s).
- Encourage them to make connections to themselves, their ideas, or their daily lives. "What does this remind you of?" Have you ever seen a rhinoceros? Where? When? Do you think this might happen to you?"
- Break up the text into manageable chunks. After reading each chunk, ask questions and/or have your students ask you or each other questions about what they have read.

As Einstein said, "Learn from yesterday, live for today, hope for tomorrow. The important thing is to not stop questioning. Curiosity has its own reason for existing."

Types of Questions to Ask

There are different kinds of questions you might ask to keep students engaged:

- The first one is **knowledge-based**. These are simple comprehension questions to find out if your students have understood the meaning of the words and sentences.
- Second, you might ask **visualization questions**. (What does it look/feel/smell/sound/taste like?) These questions use students' prior knowledge to help them connect to the reading.
- Third, ask **creative questions.** (What might happen next?/How do they feel?/What would you do in that situation?) These questions can be a lot of fun, and you should encourage students to use their imagination.
- Finally, ask **summary questions** (Tell us in your own words what/how/where..)

All of these questions can be asked both orally and in written form. Studies[1] have shown that writing can improve reading comprehension. Students who can write a summary of a text or part of a text will comprehend the text by focusing on and connecting the main ideas; using their own words also helps them to process their thoughts.

Check out Chapter 33 - Resources for Adult Educators, for more tips on how to teach Active Reading.

Turn your students from passive readers just trying to sound out words into active and engaged bookworms.

---

1. Graham, S., & Hebert, M. A. (2010). Writing to read: Evidence for how writing can improve reading. A Carnegie Corporation Time to Act Report. Washington, DC: Alliance for Excellent Education.

Perin, D. (2002). Repetition and the informational writing of developmental students. Journal of Developmental Education, 26(1), 2–18.

26

Learning Experience Activity

BUILDS CONFIDENCE AND INTEREST

The Learning Experience Activity (LEA) is another one of my all-time favorites. It is also a fantastic "Back Pocket" activity (see Chapter 29), which can be used with any student at any time. LEA is best for one-on-one lessons; however, you can use this in a small group with a bit of creativity.

In the LEA, the student dictates a short story or memory to the teacher/tutor. It should be just 3 or 4 paragraphs. Then, the student reads back ***their own words***.

Before you begin, explain what you will do and how it will help them become better readers. Here are the steps to follow:

1. The student dictates a short story to you, and you record the **exact words.**
2. You read it back and ask, "Is this right?"
3. Ask if the student wants to make any changes in their story.
4. Ask the student to give the story a title.
5. Ask if there are any words they don't recognize. Point to specific words that aren't written phonetically and other

words that may be stumbling blocks and ask them to read them.

6. Practice duet reading several times (See Chapter 24 - Duet Reading.)
7. The student reads out loud.
8. The student copies the text.
9. Practice reading out loud for HomeFun! Review at the next lesson.

You must write down **exactly what your student says**, spelling every word correctly and only adding punctuation. We have had many debates in volunteer training sessions about whether or not to correct grammatical errors. If you are teaching your student to read, DO NOT correct their grammar. The goal is to empower students to create a story in their own words. They may speak one of the[1] 30 major dialects in the USA even though they are native speakers. It would be embarrassing and belittling to tell them that the way they speak is "wrong." However, it would also be wrong not to teach them the rules of mainstream grammar at the proper time. (See Chapter 24, Ax or Ask)

On the other hand, LEA is also an excellent exercise for ESL students. If they make errors, I suggest pointing them out and asking the student to figure out what is wrong. Always ask before giving the correct answer. By engaging students' brains, they will remember and understand better. If they do this for HomeFun, you can review it with them at the next session. Make a note to come back to the specific grammar issue at another time and do a lesson on it.

LEA's advantage is that you can use it with students at any level. Adults who have had negative school experiences will enjoy the interactivity and the fact that they are learning without traditional textbooks. Students become more comfortable with reading and build up interest and confidence because it is their own story and their own words. They learn to connect spoken and written words and discover how words can have different, precise, and personal meanings. Writing their own stories is hugely empowering and builds pride and confidence as students see their own speech in writing.

Be sure to keep a copy of all of your student's written work. You can even use LEA as a warm-up at the beginning of each tutoring session. After you have enough texts, collect and assemble the writings as a series of short stories or one longer story. Print, bind, and give it to your student as a beautiful gift.

---

1. © 2023 Atlas Language Service, Inc.Retrieved Nov. 22.2023 from https://atlasls.com/english-3-different-dialects-spoken-united-states/

27

Storytelling
ORGANIZING THOUGHTS

You may be surprised to know that adults who aren't used to reading often have trouble telling a coherent real or imaginary story. Many times, a learner has come into my office to tell me about something that happened to them, and I have difficulty understanding because their story jumps around in time and in sequence.

A fascinating study on oral narrative skills in French adults who are functionally illiterate, concluded that [1]"Individuals who have not succeeded in learning to read also have impaired oral language abilities. This may affect different aspects of communication skills to a greater or lesser extent. These results have implications for teaching written language to adult learners."

Difficulties in telling a story can also give the listener a bad impression. A person with low literacy may appear agitated, embarrassed, ashamed, lacking in self-confidence, or may be easily intimidated.

The Canadian Association of Chiefs of Police did a fascinating 18-month project called [2] ***Target Crime with Literacy***. One of the fact sheets created for the police force gives tips on how to identify people with low literacy skills. Two points in relation to storytelling particularly interested me.

Those with low literacy skills:

1. have difficulty telling a clear story; for example, they may get confused about the order of events.
2. seem to talk in circles – this thinking pattern is common among people with low literacy.

This phenomenon corresponds with what we have noticed, even when one of our learners is trying to explain something simple that happened to them.

The solution is to teach students how to tell stories with a beginning, middle, and end. There are many fun ways to engage students while they are learning this skill. Here are some ideas:

- Give your learners the first and last lines of a story. For example, the beginning of the story could be:" It was a cold, dark, snowy day in the middle of winter, and I was on the bus." And the ending could be: "In spite of the horrible weather, this day turned out to be wonderful because I met a person who would become my best friend." Say and write these lines on the board and ensure everyone understands that they must create a coherent narrative. In a class setting, go around the room either in a circle or have each person who speaks call on the next one. Write down what the learners dictate to you. If the story gets incoherent or confusing, ask questions and review what they have already said.. Remind them that something has to happen to get to the conclusion that you have already given them. This is also fun to do one-on-one.

- Use semantic mapping to produce ideas. For example, explain that they are going to write a story about dogs. Draw a circle in the middle of the board and then branch out as in this image. Write the word "DOGS" in the middle of the semantic map. Brainstorm categories and then vocabulary with your learners. Guide them to come up with creative ideas.

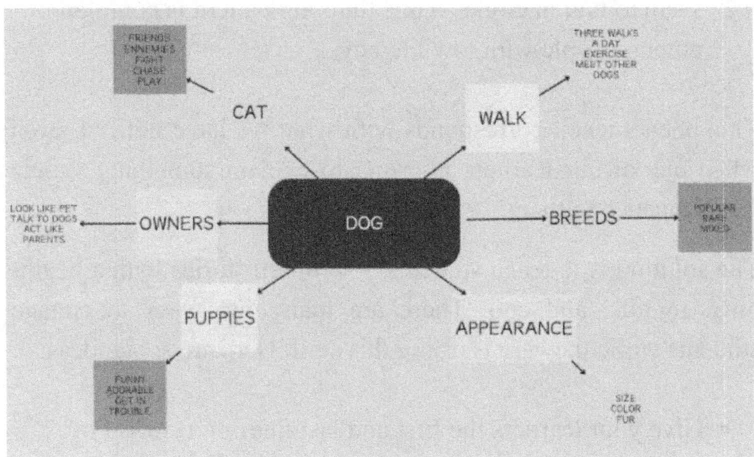

- Using the LEA technique (Chapter 26), have your learner dictate a story. The story must have a beginning, a middle, and an end! If you teach a class with more than one teacher, it would be fun to break into groups and see what each group creates. It is necessary to have a teacher guide them if this is the first time you are doing this type of exercise.

Showing a picture or a painting is also an entertaining way to inspire a story. A picture that illustrates people is always inspiring. First, discuss the picture and ask all the questions about who, what, where, when, how, and why. Write notes on the board if you are in a classroom or on a piece of paper if you are one-on-

one. Then, give the instruction for your learner(s) to write a story with a beginning, middle, and end. There are many more ways to inspire your students; however, the main goal is that they always have a structure to their stories. Using the LEA technique, they can keep copies of their work and see their improvement as storytellers.

---

1. Eme, Elsa & Lacroix, Agnès & Almecija, Yves. (2010). Oral Narrative Skills in French Adults Who Are Functionally Illiterate: Linguistic Features and Discourse Organization. Journal of speech, language, and hearing research : JSLHR. 53. 1349-71. 10.1044/1092-4388(2010/08-0092).
2. Retrieved on Nov.22,2023 from http://www.en.copian.ca/library/research/police/factsheets/toc.htm

28

Take a Phonics Break

TEACHING PHONICS IN CONTEXT

Adult learners who are at a very low level of literacy should start their adventure into the written word with a basic phonics course. However, most learners already have some basic knowledge of phonics. Since written English is so different from the way we speak, learners get confused, and why shouldn't they? Even seasoned readers may sometimes make mistakes. The famous poem attributed to T S Watt[1], points out the inconsistencies of our language.

I take it you already know
of tough and bough and cough and dough?
Others may stumble, but not you
On hiccough, thorough, slough, and through?
Well done! And now you wish, perhaps
To learn of less familiar traps?

Beware of heard, a dreadful word
That looks like beard and sounds like bird.
And dead; it's said like bed, not bead;
For goodness sake, don't call it deed!

Watch out for meat and great and threat,
(they rhyme with suite and straight and debt)

A moth is not a moth in mother.
Nor both in bother, broth in brother.
And here is not a match for there.
And dear and fear for bear and pear.
And then there's dose and rose and lose-

Just look them up-and goose and choose.
And cork and work and card and ward,
And font and front and word and sword.
And do and go, then thwart and cart.
Come, come, I've hardly made a start.

A dreadful language? Why, man alive,
I'd learned to talk it when I was five,
And yet to write it, the more I tried
I hadn't learned it at sixty-five!

Obviously, you can't teach everything in one lesson! I came up with the idea of doing what I call ***Phonics Breaks.*** These are short breaks to point out similarities and differences when they come up in lessons and are of immediate interest to your learners.

Let's say the word "cough" is in a text you are reading, and your student stumbles over it. This is a perfect time to announce***: " Phonics Break!"***

Phonic breaks need to be fun and engaging. Start by writing the word cough where your student can see it. Ask if they know any other words with a **sound** like the final f in cough. They may come up with words like off, cuff, puff or huff, fill, feet. Or possibly words like phone or graph. Write these words in separate lists, then explain that although they may sound similar, the spelling is different. **While this may be frustrating or confusing to them, they must memorize these spellings.** I usually throw my hands up in despair and tell them I wasn't the inventor of the English language, but I am there to help them decipher it. In this case, you are teaching them that the sound 'F" may be written using gh, ph, f, or ff.

Start writing a few more words with "gh" such as rough, tough, etc. Encourage your student to find more. Ask them to write or say sentences with these words to help them remember. Then do echo and/or duet reading. Feel free to make up any quick game using the words, maybe a dictation with silly sentences, or play Hangman using the words in the list. Follow up during your next session with some handouts. (See Chapter 33 - Resources).

You can also plan your phonics breaks ahead of time if you know your student's reading levels and stumbling blocks. Look through the text you are reading and prepare for one or two breaks.

The trick is to continually review, review, and review. When a new word comes up with a sound that you have already worked on, give your student time to remember. Teacher hold back! Remember that no matter how tempting it is or how much time you spend, it is important to bite your tongue and not give the answer right away. While the student is thinking, their neurons start firing off, and I believe that this action helps to stimulate their memory! Make sure your student writes down all the new words that they learn. Many recent[2] research studies have shown that writing (not typing) strengthens memory and recall.

---

1. Retrieved from English WIki on Nov. 23,2023 https://www.enwiki.org/w/English_pronunciation_poems

This is ultimately attributed to T S Watt (1954), Brush up on your English with Hints on Pronunciation for visiting Foreigners, from the Manchester Guardian.

2. Retrieved from ScienceNewsExplores, Nov.26,2023, Handwriting beats typing when it comes to taking class notes (snexplores.org)

29

Back Pocket Exercises

OH NO, WHAT CAN I DO?

It happens to every teacher. You are about to teach your class or your student, and you don't have a lesson plan, or the one you prepared isn't going to work, or it's too short, or you forgot your materials at home, or maybe you are subbing. No need to panic. First of all, don't make excuses or let the class know that your lesson is not all ready to go! Fake it till you make it! Here are a few exercises that you can literally pull out of your back pocket, and all you require is paper and pencil, a whiteboard, and a smattering of imagination.

Warm-up

First, a little warm-up while you are deciding what to do in the class! If you are subbing and/or you have a large class and can't remember everyone's name or just want to get to know your students better, start with this fun and engaging warm-up activity. Ask a student to tell you their first name and something they like such as a color, food, hobby, sport, ice cream flavor, city, etc.). Then go around the room asking each person to repeat all the names and items in order and then add theirs. Once you have gone around the room, give them a ball (real or imaginary) which they throw around the room, first saying their name and item and then the other person's, and throw the ball to the other person.

While they are playing the game, you choose what you will do for the rest of the class from the options listed below. Remember to tell the class why you are doing the next activity. After this short icebreaker, write on the board: "At the end of this session, you will be able to....", then add your objective.

Activity: Semantic Mapping (Chapter 27, Storytelling)

Remember? This activity involves creating a semantic map with your students around a topic. Depending on your class and what you want to teach them, you might choose one of these objectives:

- Practice reading and writing adjectives or adverbs to enhance their writing
- Write a story with a beginning, middle, and end
- Write in a specific verb form
- Students make up a story and write questions about it (See Chapter 25 on Active Reading for question ideas.)

Activity: Let's move

This is great for recharging students' energy levels or keeping them engaged. Play a game that uses movement. It could be Hokey Pokey, Simon Says, or any other game that will get them to move. For example, if you choose Simon Says, your objective could be to learn to read and write body parts.

Start by drawing a basic human body form (stick figures are fine) on the board or paper. Ask students to dictate the names of each body part and write them in the appropriate spot. Do duet and or echo reading to help them remember what the words look like. Then play Simon Says to help kinesthetic learners remember the connections between the written word and the body part. A variation would be to say, "Touch Your..." and point to the word. Then erase the drawing of the body and just leave the words. Continue pointing to the word on the board and have them touch that body part. Let students also have a turn being Simon!

Activity: Stressed Words

Adult literacy students often read in a monotone, sounding out the words as they go. It is important for them to read with expression. As native speakers, they automatically put the correct stress on a word in everyday conversations. However, it is essential for them to understand how the meaning of a sentence can change depending on where the stress occurs.

The objective? Be able to read out loud with meaning and expression.

Write this sentence on the board:

"I didn't say she stole the money." The normal stress would be on the negative, "didn't," and the verb "stole." (Go ahead and say it aloud!) Now have students read this sentence stressing the other words and discuss how that might change the meaning. Then, alone or in groups, have students write their own sentences and challenge the others to say them, first in a "normal" way and then in as many different ways as possible.

Activity: Storywriting

Here is another example of a quick and fun exercise that we explained in detail in Chapter 27, "Storytelling". You make up the first and last line of a story. Divide the class into groups and have each group write or tell the other group their story. Then have the students ask each other all kinds of questions. You can also do this as an LEA (Chapter 26) and then have students copy the story that they have dictated to you.

The objective? Be able to write/tell a story with a beginning, middle, and end.

Activity: Tongue Twisters

You will actually need to memorize a couple of tongue twisters for this one. Students read tongue twisters faster and faster. Check out Chapter 33 with some resources to find fun tongue twisters. You can ask your students to write their own as well!

The objective? Be able to read with fluency and expression.

Activity: Spelling Bee

This is a fun way to review sight words. Start by brainstorming all the words that students may see in the street. Make a list of them. Practice duet/echo reading and then have students copy them from the board. When they have finished, review your list on the board one more time and then erase it.

Divide students into two or three groups and give them each a space on the board to write. Or give each team a piece of paper. Students line up, and you give them one of the words you have just studied. The first person on each team writes the word on the board or on the paper. Do not correct. Give the second word, and the second person writes it down. When you have gone through all of the vocabulary, each team corrects the lists of the other team based on what they copied from the board. The team with the most correct words wins! If you still have time, have the teams or individuals write sentences with these words.

The objective? Be able to read common words in the street.

Hopefully, you will make room in YOUR back pocket for these activities and will be inspired to create more! Remember, whatever you do, HAVE FUN!

30

Digital Literacy

HOW THE COVID PANDEMIC AFFECTED LOW-LITERACY ADULTS

Before COVID-19 hit, we had a lively, interactive program with eight reading classes a week and 20 to 30 students coming daily to learn how to read. It was like a big family, everyone helping each other. Noisy, fun and comfortable.

Then came March 2020 and the Covid pandemic.

The next day, we sent everyone home for what we hoped would be a short period of time. It wasn't. After a few weeks, we realized that we needed to put all the reading classes online. Although we had a handful of students following our digital literacy classes, which we started at the end of 2018, none of our students had mastered digital skills; a few had started to learn the basics. Most of them didn't have their own computers or access to the internet at home.

We were able to lend computers to some of our students, but then came the challenge of teaching - over the phone - how to turn on the computer and connect to the internet! Many of our volunteer tutors also needed to learn how to teach online.

We started by teaching the tutors. They had to learn how to share screens, create whiteboards, and help their students navigate on their side of the screen. Some of our older volunteer tutors resisted for a while; however, their desire to help our students got stronger, and nearly all of the class teachers overcame their own digital challenges.

It was a long process, and many of our volunteers jumped in to help. I remember working with one student, trying to teach her how to open Zoom. There were three of us on Zoom: me and two tutors. She was talking to us on her phone while trying to read the instructions on her computer. Her reading level was just over first grade. After about an hour, she said, "There's one word I don't understand." "Spell it to us!" and she did. The word was "download". She didn't understand what it meant either. Ten minutes later she was able to download the Zoom application to her computer. All of us on that call remember the joy on her face when she saw us online. It was the first time she had ever been able to communicate in this way. She became an excellent participant and was a leader in encouraging other students to join the online classes.

Joining online classes was a lifesaver for many of our students who would have been home alone and isolated. It was a long, lonely period for others who couldn't connect to the internet.

This account shows the importance of digital literacy. Teaching it, though, in-person or online, can be extremely demanding and calls for a lot of patience from the instructors. Adults with low literacy levels have more difficulty learning to use computers than those who can easily read and follow written instructions, such as messages about downloading, uploading, and even where to click to find information. They also need to learn to read the keyboard and understand words like "insert," "delete," and "backspace."

We recommend teaching typing for at least 15 to 20 minutes at every lesson. This kinesthetic learning experience helps develop muscle memory. In an in-person classroom setting, you need to provide a computer for each person and at least two or even three teachers so that individuals can get help without slowing down the whole class.

Students can play many fun games to learn how to use a mouse, which is easier than starting with a touchpad. Do you remember the first time you tried to use a mouse? It is a cognitive exercise which requires a great deal of concentration. Students need to learn all the functions, such as copy and paste, drag and drop, clicking on objects, and so on.

There are very few existing courses for computer skills for adults with low literacy levels. Teachers need to be patient, creative, and to help each person at their own level. Check Chapter 33 for resources.

And our students who followed online classes for over a year? They improved their reading levels and learned to be more confident using technology. Now, they all come to our weekly in-person digital literacy classes, where their skills are constantly improving.

31

Have a Robust Training Program for Volunteers

VOLUNTEERS COME TO HELP OTHERS AND STAY BECAUSE OF WHAT THEY RECEIVE.

The United States Bureau of Labor did a study in 2017 that looked at volunteering in the US from 2016-2017. They found that 23%, nearly one-fourth of the volunteers, chose to teach or tutor. [1]

In 2019, 32,772,431 male volunteers contributed roughly 3.0 billion hours of service, and 44,614,636 female volunteers contributed roughly 3.9 billion hours of service.[2] If the above percentages were still true in 2019, one-fourth would be around 19,000,000 people volunteering to teach either adults or children. How many knew how to teach and, more specifically, teach adults? I couldn't find any statistics on how many had been trained to teach adults. From my own experience, there are very few. However, many retired school teachers do join Literacy Chicago's volunteer team. Learning how to teach adults is why a robust pre-service training program is essential.

Who makes the best tutors to teach literacy skills? People who are passionate about helping others learn to read and write, who have at least a high school level of education, and who have an abundance of patience. Excellent communication skills are essential, and knowing how to use computer technology is also helpful. If you are dependable, interested in other cultures and peoples' stories, willing to work with program staff to provide respectful and interesting learning experiences, and ready to have fun and take joy in seeing your students learn, then you will be a wonderful volunteer! Need help finding a good place to volunteer? Check out the resource page on the Proliteracy website, the leading resource and champion for adult education and literacy worldwide.[3]

Any organization that uses volunteers to teach adults to read needs a thorough training program. Most training programs are 12 to 15 hours. Literacy Chicago's training program has changed from an intensive in-person 12-hour training to a 15-hour hybrid one, with time between sessions for future tutors to do HomeFun. Training has to be fun to make it memorable.

Surprisingly, the hybrid model is much better than the one we used before the Covid pandemic. The first two sessions are on Zoom, and before each session, trainee volunteers do some reading, watch videos, and do quizzes on our LMS, CANVAS[4]. By giving trainees HomeFun to do on their own before class, they come to the sessions already very engaged and ready to jump in. By the time we meet for half a day in-person, everyone knows each other, and the atmosphere is quite relaxed. Everyone is looking forward to meeting each other - in person!

Our training is partly informational and partly hands-on. We teach all the techniques described in this book, do a simulated practice, answer questions, debate ideas, and practice lesson planning. At the end of the training, volunteers receive their certificates and are assigned a student to tutor or a class to teach.

If you are managing your organization's volunteer team, following up with your volunteers after the first few lessons is important to see if they have questions. Ensure they feel comfortable coming to you with questions and be ready to offer suggestions. Provide resources for them to find lesson plans and ideas. There are many excellent materials available online. Check Chapter 33 for a list of some that I find particularly useful and engaging.

---

1. Retrieved from U.S Bureau of Labor Statistics, https://www.bls.gov/opub/mlr/2020/article/making-volunteer-work-visible-supplementary-measures-of-work-in-labor-force-statistics.htm
2. Retrieved from Americorps, https://www.americorps.gov/sites/default/files/document/Volunteering_in_America_Demographics_508.pdf
3. Retrieved from Proliteracy, https://www.proliteracy.org/get-involved/volunteer#
4. https://www.instructure.com/canvas/login/free-for-teacher

32

Accelerated Learning for All

CHANCE ENCOUNTER OPENS DOORS TO LITERACY

While writing this book, I have had the immense privilege of working with a brilliant educator, Sunita Gandhi, who lives in Lucknow, India. I would be remiss not to acknowledge her revolutionary way of teaching the basics of reading in 90 hours: ALfA, Accelerated Learning for All.

In the summer of 2021, Milita Halder, a member of Dr. Sunita Ghandi's Global Dream team, contacted me and asked me to be a guest speaker on their YouTube Channel, DEVI Sansthan[1]. I was a guest on two programs[2]. More importantly, I met people halfway across the globe who share my passion - changing lives through literacy. This one action has already indirectly changed the lives of a group of adults in Chicago, and we hope it can inspire positive change for hundreds of thousands more.

Let me share parts of an article I wrote for the inaugural edition of Devi Sansthan's **10 X GOOD Magazine,** published in June 2023.[3]

"Traditionally there have been two widely debated approaches to teaching reading. The first is the 'Whole Language' method,

where words are simply memorized as whole units. The second approach involves teaching 'Phonics,' which focuses on the relationship between letters or groups of letters and the sounds they represent. One of the challenges, as explained by Dr. Gandhi, is that these methods often start from the unknown and progress toward the known. The sight word method involves memorizing the visual appearance of a word without understanding its meaning, while the phonics method uses unfamiliar symbols (letters) to connect to sounds that are also unknown, as in "b" says BEE. [4]

Dr. Gandhi recognized the need to create an alternative approach to reading instruction that starts with what learners already know, connecting it to sounds, and then introducing the corresponding symbols (letters). In the ALfA method for literacy (Accelerating Learning for All), learners begin by looking at a picture of a common object and are asked to identify the FIRST sound of the word. They are then shown the letter that represents that sound. No emphasis is placed on the name of the letter or its place in the alphabet. The goal is to connect known pictures to the first sounds of these pictures and add the known sounds to make words from the beginning. The letter is shown as a sound symbol.

The ALfA method consists of two concise books, enabling learners to grasp the method within just 45 work or school days with one lesson a day. The first book teaches the sounds of consonants and vowels, while the second introduces [5]*digraphs and delves into more complex reading, including short stories and poetry. Astonishingly, Dr. Gandhi explained that learners can read a newspaper within two months of utilizing this method. This revelation astonished me, given that I have witnessed the struggles faced by our adult learners, whose progress is often slow.*

Several aspects of ALfA immediately appealed to me. First and foremost, it is an affordable program that can be accessed online, making it economically feasible. Additionally, ALfA employs pair work, enabling learners to work together and provide positive feedback, fostering a collaborative learning environment. Most importantly, ALfA is designed to be enjoyable for teachers and learners. It adopts a student-centric approach where learners have agency in their own learning process. Teachers are facilitators, demonstrating the method and allowing learners to engage in activities independently."

After visiting Dr. Gandhi in Lucknow and seeing the ALfA method in use, I am convinced that this method is the future of teaching the basics of reading. Literacy Chicago did the first pilot program with adults in the US in April 2023, and the results have been spectacular.

This method is especially useful for students who speak English as a first language and who have no preconceived ideas about how reading should be taught or learned. Shockingly, some adults in the USA never learned the alphabet, even if they had some schooling. Students who first learned the sight word method or the phonic method need to change their mindsets. Once they embrace ALfA, they are amazed at how quickly they can learn to read.

---

1. https://www.youtube.com/@DEVISansthan
2. See my interviews here: https://www.youtube.com/live/nitjVV43-Mo?feature=share, https://www.youtube.com/live/tUSqsOLoZSA?feature=share
3. https://10xgood.org/devi-sansthan-magazine.html, at Pages 28-31.
4. By this I mean that it is confusing to teach the name of a letter, versus the sound it makes. Although we pronounce the letter B as "bee", when you see a word such as "babe" we don't say "bee-AA-bee".
5. Definition of Digraph:a combination of two letters representing one sound, such as as "ck" or "qu"

33

Resources

HOW TO CHOOSE?

There are so many online resources for lesson planning and materials that sometimes you can spend hours looking for just the right article, exercise, or idea for your lesson. To get you started, I want to share some of the resources I go to first!

Hi-Lo Books (High Interest-Low Level Readability)

- www.yalsa.ala.org/thehub/2016/09/07/books-stuff-happens-exploration-hilo-searching/
- www.fbmarketplace.org/see-all-books/topic/reluctant-readers/hi-lo-reading

Poetry

- Download a free copy of "Small Talk" by Carolyn Graham www.pdfcookie.com/download/carolyn-graham-small-talk-more-jazz-chants-7rv3p04zd92d

  ○ Note: Website states:(https://pdfcookie.com/) *This*

document was uploaded by user and they confirmed that they have the permission to share it.

Create Fun Online Games

- Kahoot: https://kahoot.com/
- Quizziz: https://quizizz.com/?lng=en
- Create your own Jeopardy game: www.superteachertools.com/jeopardyx/index.php

Make your own Crossword puzzles

- www.education.com/worksheet-generator/reading/crossword-puzzle/
- https://crosswordlabs.com/

Teaching Active Reading

- Reading Instructional Strategies: Resources for Adult Educators: https://illinois.pbslearningmedia.org/collection/ristrat/
- LINCS is a government website which provides many free resources and online courses for adult educator and also a "Learner Center" that has resources specifically for students. https://lincs.ed.gov/

Some specific links from Lincs

Teaching Adults How to Summarize

- https://lincs.ed.gov/state-resources/federal-initiatives/teal/guide/teachsumm
- https://lincs.ed.gov/sites/default/files/10_TEAL_Self_Reg_Strat_Dev_0.pdf

Tongue Twisters

- www.mondly.com/blog/2019/08/23/71-best-tongue-twisters-to-perfect-your-english-pronunciation/
- www.engvid.com/english-resource/50-tongue-twisters-improve-pronunciation/

Short Leveled Texts

- **Read Works**: Free content, curriculums, and tools from Kindergarten to 12th-grade levels. Although this is geared toward K-12 schools, many lesson plans are fairly sophisticated. www.readworks.org/
- **Literacy Minnesota:** Excellent free content for adult and children educators, including lesson plans, tips on teaching, phonics, webinars, and much more. www.literacymn.org/educator-resources

Digital Literacy

- **Byte Back:** is an excellent resource for learning how to type. It is simple, straightforward, and very accessible for adults. https://byteback.org/scholars-alumni/typing-tutorial/
- **GFC Global:** Free Microsoft Office, email, to reading, math, and more than 200 topics, including over 2,300 lessons, 2,000 videos, and 50 interactives and games. Excellent digital literacy mouse exercises and self-taught course. https://edu.gcfglobal.org/en/
- **Public Library Association:** DigitalLearn.org is an excellent site for free digital support and training. There are short courses for everything from the basics to more advanced topics such as online safety, shopping, job search skills, and social media.

More 33 Ways!

If you enjoyed this book, check out one or more of the books in the series:

"33 Ways Not to Screw Up Consulting"
"33 Ways Not to Screw Up Your Business Emails"
"33 Ways Not to Screw Up Cybersecurity"
"33 Ways Not to Screw Up Your Financial Life"
"33 Ways Not to Screw Up Creative Entrepreneurship"
"33 Ways Not to Screw Up Journalism"
"33 Ways Not to Screw Up Negotiations"
"33 Ways Not to Screw Up HR"
"33 Ways Not to Screw Up Hiring Great Talent"
"33 Ways Not to Screw Up Your Business Podcast"
"33 Ways Not to Screw Up a Thought Leadership Book"

And finally, check out: 33WaysSeries.com

Acknowledgments

Writing this book has been a challenge and a journey. I was able to stay on track and get to the end thanks to Karen Fredrickson, Master Tutor Trainer and volunteer at Literacy Chicago. She brainstormed ideas with me, encouraged me, and proofread this book in great detail - twice! I want to give my appreciation and thanks to two other Literacy Chicago volunteers who proofread this book. Alice Ginsburgh, who had to adapt her proofreading experience from Word to Google Docs and who challenged me with excellent questions, from ideas and grammar to copywriting issues. Betty Hurder, who has been a volunteer for many years, also went through the final document as well, putting in all the missing commas (her specialty!).

Many thanks also to my friend Alison Duncombe, with whom I have danced in our NIA class for over ten years. Alison read this book with interest even though she doesn't work in the world of literacy. She caught and questioned me on everything that wasn't perfectly clear to someone in a different field.

I am also grateful to Richard Dominguez, Executive Director at Literacy Chicago. He has always listened to me, encouraged me, and allowed me to work on this book during office hours. The best "boss" anyone could ask for!

Thank you to Melissa G. Wilson, bestselling author, Founder, and President of Networlding Publishing. The "33 Ways Not to Screw Up..." series is her brainchild, and she encouraged me to write this book. Without Melissa, all these ideas would still be in my head!

I hope you have found some new ideas in this book that will help you in your tutoring or teaching. If you have any questions, comments, or remarks, I would love to hear from you on LinkedIn. linkedin.com/in/joannetelserfrere

About the Author

Hailing from the vibrant city of Chicago, Joanne is a natural-born adventurer passionate about exploring the world. Her journey has taken her across the globe, leading her to live and work in diverse countries such as France, Pakistan, Egypt, and Qatar. Fluent in French with a smattering of Arabic, Joanne has navigated her way through various cultural landscapes, embracing each experience along the way.

Joanne's career has been as diverse as her travels, spanning the realms of education, radio, television, and even brain training. Today, her adventurous spirit finds expression in the realm of literacy.

As the Director of Program Development at Literacy Chicago, where she has been since 2016, Joanne brings together her extensive skill set acquired over the years to craft innovative and captivating programs for adult students. She also oversees the Volunteer Tutor program at Literacy Chicago, where she leads a team of more than 150 enthusiastic volunteers dedicated to positively impacting students' lives.

Beyond her professional endeavors, Joanne's interests encompass acting, storytelling, and an insatiable love for reading. Her greatest joy, however, lies in leveraging the power of literacy to effect transformative change in the lives of others.

Made in the USA
Monee, IL
09 April 2025